BENAUD

ALSO BY BRIAN MATTHEWS

The Receding Wave: Henry Lawson's Prose (1972)

Louisa (1987)

Quickening and Other Stories (1989)

Oval Dreams (1991)

Magpie: A Novel (with Peter Goldsworthy; 1992)

Federation (1999)

A Fine and Private Place (2000)

As the Story Goes (2001)

The Temple Down the Road (2003)

Manning Clark: A Life (2008)

BENAUD

AN APPRECIATION

BRIAN MATTHEWS

TEXT PUBLISHING MELBOURNE AUSTRALIA

textpublishing.com.au

The Text Publishing Company
Swann House
22 William Street
Melbourne Victoria 3000
Australia

First published by The Text Publishing Company 2016

Book design by Imogen Stubbs
Cover photograph by Harry Martin / Fairfax Syndication
Typeset by J&M Typesetting

Printed and bound in Australia by Griffin Press, an accredited ISO/NZS 1401:2004 Environmental Management System printer

National Library of Australia Cataloguing-in-Publication entry
ISBN: 9781925355581 (paperback)
ISBN: 9781925410013 (ebook)
Creator: Matthews, Brian (Brian Ernest), author.
Title: Benaud : an appreciation / by Brian Matthews.
Subjects: Benaud, Richie, 1930–2015. Cricket players—Australia—Biography.
Television journalists—Australia—Biography.
Dewey Number: 796.358092

For Psiche and Philip Hughes
and
Sue and Rick Hosking

CONTENTS

CONTENTS

PROLOGUE

The Well-dressed Cricketer

'Whether diving desperately to make his ground, leaping high
in the gully for a catch or just picking himself up after some
acrobatic fielding, Richie Benaud always looked the part—trim,
in control, somehow always uncreased, unstained, impeccable.'
MICHAEL CHARLTON, ABC cricket commentary

The team which had the doubtful benefit of my part-time
bowling and occasionally slightly more convincing batting
was the Adelaide Graduates—a group drawn mostly from the
University of Adelaide's Economics Department, with the odd
Flinders University academic, like me, thrown in. We played in
and lost two grand finals in the five or six years I was with them,
so it wasn't as if we lacked talent. Yet our team list was remarkable not so much for performances as for fame of a certain,
non-cricketing kind.

One of the opening batsmen was Geoff Harcourt, a professor of economics at the University of Adelaide and later a

Cambridge academic of great distinction. Our wicketkeeper was Keith Hancock, foundation professor of economics at Flinders University, and later vice-chancellor. Dick Blandy, a top-order batsman, became a professor of economics at Flinders and later the head of the National Institute of Labour Studies. Tony Hosking was an up-and-coming geologist. And then there were various teachers, writers and eccentrics. It was a wonderful team to be a part of, in a good competition: the cricket was serious and of a fairly high standard but the Graduates also knew how to enjoy themselves on and off the field and, grand-final losses notwithstanding, the end-of-year dinner was legendary.

The place was our home ground, the beautiful Waite Oval in suburban Adelaide. The time: late October and the first round of the 1968–69 season for teams in the south-suburban competition. In the field were the Adelaide Graduates CC, having won the toss and put 'the other mob' in. On the back foot at 7 for not many were our opponents. While we of the Graduates were getting changed rumours had circulated that the opposition were a couple of players short—not an unusual problem for amateur teams at the start of a new season—and that they'd scoured the nearby Edinburgh Hotel for stand-ins. This was why it seemed like a good toss to win.

And so, with another batsman falling to the pace of our strike bowler, Tony Hosking—who was the object of great interest among several grade clubs—in came their number eight. He was the quintessential cricketer—at least to look at—as he strode out to face the crisis in the middle. His whites were immaculate, his pads clean and bright, his cap balanced, just short of jaunty. He carried his gloves in one hand, bat in the other.

He was one of those batsmen who take block before ceremoniously and rather slowly putting on the gloves. And having done that, he was also one of those batsmen who then gaze intently round the field, pointing the bat at each fieldsman as if mentally burning the image into his memory. Finally, he settled into his stance and faced the storming Hosking…whose searing yorker took the middle and off stumps right out of the ground.

Walking off with the same panache he'd displayed on arrival only minutes earlier, the well-dressed cricketer met our deep fine leg, Dick Maguire, as the fieldsman headed to the centre to celebrate. 'Bad luck, mate,' said the amiable Maguire. 'First hit of the season, eh?'

The bloke looked at him, stupefied. 'First hit ever,' he said, and continued gratefully towards the anonymity of the sheds.

PART I

1

THE MASTER OF CONTROL

Point–Counterpoint

'He showed just enough emotion to let everyone know
he was pleased, and that was it.' RICHIE BENAUD
on leg-spinner Stuart McGill's control

On 18 February 2010 I wrote to Richie Benaud to propose my idea of writing his biography. 'Dear Richie Benaud,' I began, after some agonising over the stiff 'Dear Mr Benaud' or the too matey 'Dear Richie'. I wrote truthfully, 'I've been pondering for the past month or so how to get in touch with you without being or appearing intrusive…and decided on a good old-fashioned personal letter.'

I began by quoting from a piece of reminiscence I had written but failed to finish years earlier about the Fourth Test at Old Trafford in 1961, which went some way to explaining why I was keen to write about him. I then got down to the business of trying to sell myself to him. To do this I thought it necessary to outline my claims and qualifications in the dicey art of biography. I accomplished this exercise after thirty or more attempts and finished up with a few more relevant personal details, such as my sports history—a modest proficiency at Australian Rules football, cricket, squash, badminton and long-distance running, including five marathons. I even added my best time.

I concluded the letter by saying, 'I hope you can look with some tolerance on this proposal and that you will excuse its length.' There didn't seem to be much point in making a half-hearted pitch. 'I look forward to discussing it further with you whenever and wherever suits you best.'

Less than two weeks later I had my answer—brief, courteous and to the point, on an A4 sheet headed in bold sixteen-point capitals:

RICHIE BENAUD OBE

Dear Brian Matthews

Thank you for your letter concerning the Old Trafford Test of 1961 and the fact that you have spoken to Penguin about a biography of me.

My situation has always been, and will not change, that anyone can write a biography on anyone else but that I don't wish to play any part in it at all. Every so often I receive a request similar to yours and the answer remains the same.

Best of luck with your endeavours and your writing.

Yours sincerely

[signed]

Richie Benaud

This was disappointing but not altogether surprising. I had heard from both authoritative and dubious sources that Benaud had strong views about such ventures, views—if you believed the full gamut—that ranged from polite disinclination, through determined rejection, to a J. D. Salinger-like reclusiveness. Much more reliably, I knew about my friend Rob Steen's experience.

A stylish, experienced and highly regarded sports journalist for the *Guardian*, the *Independent*, the *Financial Times*, the Melbourne *Age*, the *Sunday Telegraph* and the *Sunday Times*, where he was deputy sports editor, Steen is now a senior lecturer in sports journalism at the University of Brighton. His biography of the mercurial English top-order batsman David Gower won the 1995 Cricket Society Literary Award, and he is the biographer of the celebrated West Indian opening batsman Desmond Haynes. He also had an interest in and wrote about boxing, but cricket was and remains his first love, and so it was not surprising that he should have been attracted to the prospect of a Richie Benaud biography.

Benaud was as familiar a figure to English people as he was to Australians. By the time Steen was beginning to gather his biographical forces in the early 1990s, Benaud was as well known on English television as Michael Parkinson. Those with longer memories knew him as an exciting young all-rounder, a figure as charismatic and attractive as his compatriot Keith Miller—and in many ways not unlike him—and as a brilliantly innovative and tactical captain. The cricket writer Ian Wooldridge saw him as

> arguably the finest captain Australia has ever had at any sport. Don Bradman may have been more obviously ruthless but when it came to playing mind-games and inspiring teams to play way above themselves, none compared with Richie Benaud, who never lost a Test Cricket series…He orchestrated probably the most thrilling Test series ever played, Australia v West Indies in 1960–61, which began with the first Tied Test in history and ended with 80,000 people lining the streets of Melbourne to send a narrowly defeated West Indian team on their way home. A trained journalist while reaching the top at cricket, Benaud needed no Press relations back-up team. He handled the media himself, never allowing the historic Pom–Aussie rivalry to run into anything approaching…crude, rude anti-English rhetoric.

All in all, as Rob Steen recounted the story to me over a few beers in the Queen's Larder near the University of London, the project looked like a winner. It lost that promising appearance when, beginning a pattern which years later I would recognise, Benaud replied to Steen's letter inviting co-operation with a firm refusal. As Steen recalled, 'According to Richie Benaud, one biography a lifetime was enough, adding that his attitude did not reflect any "false modesty".' Steen wondered, then, if Benaud might have an autobiographical work already planned and was taking care not to 'queer his own pitch'. He had another shot, however.

'[My] persistence…led to a private audience during the tea interval of a NatWest Trophy match in deepest Essex. That was when the Ice Man cometh. "I stand by what I wrote to you," he said before I had a chance to draw on my limited powers of persuasion. "One biography in a lifetime is enough for anyone." I did not think it would do my cause much good to point out that, in his case, biography had short-changed its readers. Instead, I made a mild show of defiance, lamenting his decision but asserting I would carry on regardless, believing I could still cobble together something worthwhile.'

Steen was underrating himself. It would not have been 'cobbled' and it would certainly have been 'worthwhile' if he had been able to continue. But in the ensuing months the Benaud fortress began to look impregnable, as each of Steen's courteous approaches to it bounced right back.

A letter to Lynton Taylor, Executive Vice-President of Business Affairs, Nine Network Australia Ltd, attracted this reply on 23 December 1992:

Dear Rob,
Thank you for your letter to Mr [Kerry] Packer of 15th

December. It would not be appropriate for Mr Packer to make himself available to provide an interview for your proposed biography of Richie Benaud. We respect Richie's decision and on this basis we think it would be inappropriate for us to be involved in the provision of material.

On the very same day Max Walker replied on Channel Nine's Wide World of Sports letterhead with the same amiability that he projected as a television commentator:

Dear Rob,

Thank you very much for your letter. I understand how difficult it is to research and write a work such as yours and I wish you a most satisfying journey with a successful book. I feel it would be in my best interests to decline your invitation on the basis that a contribution from me could personally compromise my Nine Network work relationship with Richie Benaud. Good luck and Merry Christmas to you.

The former Australian Test captain and, at the time, coach of the Australian XI, Bob Simpson, reacted as he had never done when watching the ball hurtling towards him in the slips: he ducked. 'Thank you for your letter and request to assist with your proposed book on Richie Benaud. Unfortunately I will be in New Zealand with the Australian team at the time of your proposed visit so will not be able to see you. I wish you well with your project.'

The former Australian Test captain Ian Craig, writing on the letterhead of The Boots Company (Australia) Pty Ltd, of which he was managing director, was more forthcoming, but worked his way to the same conclusion:

As a personal friend of Richie's your letter causes me some dilemma. I appreciate that he is a very public figure which makes his story of interest to many, but I also know that he is an intensely private person who in this case has obviously expressed a wish that his privacy be respected.

On balancing these conflicting issues I am also cognizant of the fact that publication of such a book is a commercial venture for both you and your publisher which brings no financial reward to Richie. Whether or not he needs such reward, I do feel it unfair that he should not partake in the benefits flowing from the story which he has created.

After much thought, I have decided that I should support Richie's wishes and therefore decline to contribute. I am sure others will fill in the minimum amount that I could offer but at least in taking this decision I believe I am respecting a friendship which has endured more than 40 years.

Reeling from these rapidly accumulating and depressingly similar blows, Steen could not but be in some awe of this aerogramme letter, written in a neat flowing hand, dated 29 December 1992:

> Dear Rob
>
> After having had a discussion with Richie on the subject matter of a biography, I find he is very firm in his resolve that he does not wish another one to be produced.
>
> This being so, I feel obligated to support his attitude and do not feel that I can co-operate with its production.
>
> In any case, as our careers were in different eras I have no knowledge about him that is not already public property and so could be of no help.
>
> Yours faithfully
>
> Don Bradman

The letters from Bradman and Craig arrived in Rob Steen's letterbox at Flat 2, 111 Broadhurst Gardens NW6—at one time the London residence of the Demon Bowler, Fred Spofforth—either side of New Year's Day, 1992–93, with Bradman's leading the way. For Steen they precipitated some serious thinking.

'This brought me to the question all would-be biographers must sooner or later ask themselves. Is it necessary to know your subject personally? I am still not entirely sure…Ideally one should obtain the subject's blessing and establish a rapport that enables feelings to be unlocked and memories tapped. Yet even that road may be littered with potholes.

'Richie represented the worst of both worlds. As much in the public eye in his sixties as he was in his pomp as a player, he was alive and well and set against the whole thing. If he had done something terrible, or even merely harmful, I might have been justified in refusing to respect his privacy—public duty and all that. Unfortunately, this is a person who has merely done his various jobs supremely well, a man who, moreover, has sought to protect his image with the same zeal as a Louvre security guard babysitting the *Mona Lisa*.

'My aim, however, was to examine and celebrate, not expose or soil…The worst crime anyone was prepared to accuse him of was being calculating.'

But even the face-to-face contact that, by implication, Steen valued highly as part of the biographer's approach failed him. The meeting successfully arranged after some difficulty proved not merely unsuccessful but uncomfortable. Steen, a charming man at ease in most social and formal situations, found the atmosphere discouraging.

'[Benaud's] jacket was as immaculately pressed as its wearer's image. The expression was utterly devoid of emotion, the handshake firm but cold, the eyes more glacial still. They call him the "Ice Man" because of his incredible coolness under pressure, but these first impressions indicated a more profound reason. From that moment I should have known that my quest to write a biography of Richie Benaud was doomed.'

At the other end of the process, with that doom imminent, Steen, after numerous setbacks, stonewalling and silences, writes: 'By now I had suffered the most grievous double whammy any would-be biographer can sustain. Not only had I lost faith in my capacity to capture and convey my subject, I had also mislaid my enthusiasm. To proceed would be pointless. My editor added, somewhat needlessly, that to do so would also undermine what he graciously described as my "reputation".'

And so the project lapsed, and Rob laid aside his notes and correspondence, generously digging them out twenty years on when I wrote to him seeking his help. 'None of [these events and setbacks],' he concludes, 'should reflect ill on "Benordy"—as Benaud was occasionally called in England early in his career. Everyone, no matter how famous, is entitled to their privacy.'

Bravely facing the inevitable, Steen had arrived at that literary cul-de-sac described by Richard Holmes in his brilliant memoir, *Footsteps*. 'I had come to suspect that there is something frequently comic about the trailing figure of the biographer: a sort of tramp permanently knocking at the kitchen window and secretly hoping he might be invited in for supper.' Benaud, it would seem, had glimpsed the tramp and resolved to turn politely but firmly away.

At just this time an advertisement Steen had placed in a cricket magazine bore sudden fruit. A Mrs Margaret Mullins of Withington, Manchester, wrote to say she too had been aspiring to write a Benaud biography and 'had collected material for such a book in the 1970s, with the knowledge of Richie', and

that, although she had abandoned the specifically biographical venture when Benaud wrote 'his autobiography', she had
'continued writing on cricket with the accent on Richie—detail-
ing his views, talks and activities etc, and anything about him'.
As a result she had '350–400 pages of A4 typed notes' and she
wondered 'if this would be of use, or interest' to him. But Rob
was exhausted and dispirited, and did not take up the offer.

Margaret Mullins' letter was dated 27 January 1993. In
the nearly two decades that had elapsed between then and my
reading of Rob Steen's papers and correspondence, much could
have happened. For one thing, the 350–400 A4 pages may have
been thrown out or burnt or have mouldered away in a shed
somewhere. Mrs Mullins may have disappeared. The possibilities were numerous and seemed very much in accord with Richie
Benaud's elusiveness. He would no doubt have appreciated and
applauded the evanescence, the endlessly diminishing nature
of the 'evidence'. But I had a foot soldier in Manchester, and I
wrote to him.

> In 1993 a Mrs Margaret Mullins lived at 16 Brunswick
> Road, Withington, Manchester M20 9QB. In a letter to
> Rob Steen, Mrs Mullins said she had 'collected material
> for such a book' [a biography of Benaud], in the 1970s,
> with the knowledge of Richie. She says in her letter that
> she had 'some 350–400 pages of A4 typed notes', which
> might be of interest. I don't think Rob replied because
> he was chucking the whole thing at just that time. Mrs

Margaret Mullins may have moved from Withington, or have died or be otherwise uncontactable, but if you felt like strolling up to 16 Brunswick Road sometime on behalf of a putative Benaud biographer to whom Steen has given his blessing and slender archive, it might be the start of something...Let us know what you think. I'll understand if this looks too hard.

For a while it was a bit too hard. My 'research assistant' was a busy senior academic at the University of Manchester and had many calls on his time. On the other hand, I had a certain amount of leverage because he was also my eldest son. I carefully refrained from badgering him but after a few quiet weeks I mentioned the quest among other things in an email and provoked a slightly guilty reply: 'Okay, I'll get on to this soonest.'

Sure enough, he was back in touch within a few days.

Okay, so it appears that there is no Margaret Mullins at that address you mention and has not been for some time. I haven't actually been there but am going off to examine the electoral roll. There are two candidates, however, who live quite close to Withington, and two others, further away. I have just sent identical letters to them all, asking them to get in touch if they're the one. Well, I didn't phrase it quite like that, but you know what I mean. I will also try to get to Brunswick Rd to check.

'Excellent work, and many thanks, especially for going to the trouble of writing to the suspects,' I replied, but added gloomily, 'I think the trail may be cold.' Then, after another tense interval, 'I think the trail may indeed be cold. I've had no response to those letters and suspect that if I was going to, it would have happened quite quickly. It remains to rule out the Brunswick Rd address.' So, that, for the moment, was that. Fortress Benaud had effortlessly repelled another attack.

He may or may not have been aware of it, but in being so determinedly biography-shy—with Steen twenty-odd years ago and more recently with me—Richie Benaud was bringing his own distinction to an already rather glittering line-up. George Orwell and T. S. Eliot both tried to counter prospective biographers; George Bernard Shaw did not expressly forbid the biographical act but tried to foil literary sleuths with deliberately false leads and manufactured obfuscations; and the late J. D. Salinger subverted his would-be biographer, Ian Hamilton, by refusing him access to papers and the right to quote. Shane Warne similarly blocked Paul Barry's biographical intentions by closing off as many avenues of information as he could—and they were many. When, in a face-to-face plea, Barry protested that it would be 'very hard to write a fair book if I can't talk to anyone who likes you', Warne countered, 'Then don't write it.'

But biography-averse people of no matter what distinction would not be comforted by the knowledge that attempts to limit or outsmart the life-writers almost invariably end the same way: in unauthorised biography. Despite Orwell's own embargo, several biographies appeared both before and after Sonia Orwell, as his literary executor, capitulated and attempted to stem the flow by authorising Bernard Crick. There is no official biography of T. S. Eliot, but two substantial works by Peter Ackroyd and Lyndall Gordon stand as authoritative, if unauthorised, precursors and there are many guerrillas making sporadic incursions, such as T. S. Matthews with his witty *Great Tom: Notes Towards the Definition of T. S. Eliot*. As for the Salinger–Hamilton saga, Ian Hamilton adroitly turned embargo into an industry, publishing *In Search of J. D. Salinger*—a book about his attempts to write a book about his subject. And in a different but connected way, A. J. Symons's riveting tour de force *The Quest for Corvo: An Experiment in Biography* stands as a kind of daring biographical Fodor's guide to the strange business of trying to trace someone else's life story.

'Everyone, no matter how famous, is entitled to their privacy,' Rob Steen wrote generously as he abandoned his Benaud project. They are, yet everyone, no matter how anonymous, is entitled to his or her curiosity. The private world of a person, no matter how closely guarded, is surrounded by a sort of penumbra of people's memories and opinions, events, ruling passions, public achievements and failures, published and recorded words, and so on, which are forever beyond the reach of the controlling consciousness that produced them. Like unruly witnesses of variable significance they have been released into the world and, although their chattering can be marshalled, organised, ordered this way or that, they can never be silenced.

Take the leg-break, for instance: what might we learn from the dedication someone has to bowling leg-breaks? Well, such a person is the exponent—or at least an acolyte—of not merely an aspect of a game but of an art.

The leg-break, Richie Benaud says in a short explanatory film, is 'the most complicated form of bowling'. 'Fast bowling is as it appears. Medium-pace bowling is the same. Orthodox finger-spin is difficult, but over-the-wrist spin to right-handed and left-handed batsmen is very complicated. The main thing is to keep it simple.'

'[With leg-spin] you have a very very difficult art form where the ball is going to come out of the hand in a most unorthodox fashion at a time when your body is in a very strange position—a bit like the golf swing—it's an unnatural thing. The leg-break is the most important [weapon] in an over-the-wrist spinner's armoury...He must spin it fiercely, spin it hard, and he must bowl it exactly where he wants it so it will get him out of trouble when, as is always the case, he gets himself into trouble against a good batsman.'

Asked if a leg-spin bowler should first perfect a good length, Benaud retorts, 'Forget about length. You have lots of bowlers who are just rollers. They just put the ball there. It suits them, particularly if they get a pitch that may have been prepared to help them and they can return good figures, but that's no good. It's like trying to teach a medium-pacer to become a great fast bowler. You can't do it. You've got to have the pace first...The leg-spinner must have the fierce spin and then learn to control it, and that is going to take, mind you, four years to learn that control.'

A bowler whose stock ball is the leg-break is a wrist-spinner: the anti-clockwise spin imparted is generated more by wrist action than by fingers, though the fingers play a crucial role in the process. The index and middle fingers are on the seam, and the ball is stabilised between third finger and thumb—though Benaud says the thumb is irrelevant and needn't be on the ball at all. On release, the combination of wrist and third finger produces the spin. When the ball bounces, the spin takes it from a trajectory on or about the leg stump across the right-handed batsman, towards the off side.

Of course, the amount of spin and the line of attack vary with the technique and abilities of the bowler. Shane Warne's 'ball of the century' to the English batsman Mike Gatting in 1993 (which Benaud commentated and later called 'absolutely magnificent') pitched outside the leg stump and took the off bail. No wonder Gatting could scarcely believe what had happened. When, that evening over a beer, he asked Warne, 'What happened?' the answer was, 'You just missed a leg-break, buddy.' Some leg-break.

When Shane Warne bowled early in his first-class career, the batsman standing at the non-striker's end often remarked on the hissing sound as the ball left his hand. It was spinning so hard that it sang through the air. And that, as Richie Benaud pointed out, is how it should be. You spin hard, fiercely; you rip the ball out every time you bowl the leg-break. The grip, the initially awkward, unnatural position of the ball in the bowling hand; the relative difficulty of spinning it hard but making it go where you want it to go; and the trajectory—preferably upwards as it leaves the hand—all demonstrate Benaud's emphasis that leg-spin bowling is a very difficult art.

And an art it is, taking years to perfect. Someone who spends that kind of time relentlessly, self-sacrificingly devoted to a beautiful but extraordinarily challenging art is bound to be someone of interest, someone perhaps for whom control, the central requirement of top-class spin bowling, is paramount.

Control is what Richie Benaud succeeded in mastering as one of Australia's great leg-break bowlers. So did Shane Warne, even more so, uncannily. Warne the Test cricketer sought and achieved control year after year, match after match, over after over, but off the field of play control was often lacking. Benaud's on-field control, however, was carried into his life away from cricket and magnified as the years passed. His justly famous commentary style was also, centrally, a matter of control. He spoke when he could be informative, challenging, interesting, insightful or—occasionally and usually ironically—witty. If those opportunities were not available—and during television cricket commentary they are often scarce—he remained silent.

It was one aspect of Benaud's control that Rob Steen encountered and that he interpreted as the mien of an 'ice man'; it was another aspect that I encountered in his polite but severely well-controlled response to my letter; and it was yet another version that I ran into when, given the name of a friend of the

Benauds living in France, I wrote to this man. As he wishes to remain anonymous, I will call him Paul.

I began with this message:

> Dear Paul
>
> I'm writing a book about Richie Benaud and when I mentioned this to my good friends Philip and Psiche Hughes, Philip said he thought you knew or had some connection with Richie. If that's the case and if you don't mind my intruding on you 'out of the blue' like this, I wonder if you might be willing to have some discussion online. I can tell you more about myself and my track record as a writer, if you wish, or you could ask Philip to fill you in on the details.
>
> My main idea for this book is to present and celebrate a great Australian cricketer and captain and an extraordinarily gifted cricket analyst and commentator in a way that would not be done if left to a ghost-writing journalist and in a way that Benaud himself, for obvious reasons of due modesty, cannot do, and has not done for himself in his autobiographical work, interesting though that is...

Paul's answer was swift and encouragingly generous:

> Brian, I am certainly willing to contribute my knowledge of Richie to your biography. He has been

24

a close friend since his days of being the captain of the Australian team in the sixties—and later, so has Daphne. But I don't want to cover ground that you are already familiar with. What stage have you reached so far? Can you, as you suggest, tell me more about your relationship to Richie and Daphne. Do they know you are writing about them?

I replied with the information Paul asked for, but I detected in his reply a note of caution.

> Brian, thank you for telling me more about yourself and your reasons for wanting to write a Benaud biography. My decision to participate could only be made after I had received assurance from Richie and Daphne that I would be doing so with their full approval. So I have written to them to ask the question. I ought to warn you, in case you do not know already, that anything written about Richie would be scrutinised, probably edited, by Daphne. It is her approval that you need, not Richie's. I will email you when I receive a reply to my letter.

Sensing complications that were escaping beyond my vestigial reach, I reassured him as best I could:

> Thanks Paul. I realised when I first approached you that, if you were interested, you would obviously have

to consult the Benauds. I am also aware of Daphne's rumoured role as scrutineer, editor and general literary overseer...Anyway, I look forward to hearing from you when you have contacted the Benauds and thanks again for devoting time to this 'quest'.

Paul duly contacted the Benauds and came back not only with the kind of kybosh that had knocked the biographical stuffing out of Rob Steen, but also with some advice which amounted to a less-than-veiled opinion that I should give up.

Brian, I have now heard from Richie Benaud. He has copied to me a letter he wrote you on 1 March 2010... In case you never received this I can tell you that it is very brief and tells you that 'anyone who wishes can write a biography of him' but that he will play no part in its preparation or publication.

In these circumstances I am prepared to write a one-paragraph anonymous summary of my experience of Richie's character but you could also obtain that from a long list of people close to Richie. I do not think it would add value to your proposed biography. Also, I feel that Richie's ten books are in themselves so biographical that you would have a tough time finding enough new material to fill a book. But that is just my opinion, of course...

Somewhat staggered by the assumption that I must not have heard back from Benaud and that I'd done nothing about it, I assured Paul that not only had I received the letter but that I had courteously replied to it expressing my understanding of his position but also my disappointment. As for his conviction about the futility of my task, I suggested—with suitable diffidence—that I had confronted similar difficulties in past projects and found a way through, so perhaps I'd manage this time as well, despite the formidable Benaud fortress having raised the drawbridge, shut the gates and put the word out to the surrounding countryside to beware of marauding biographers.

True to his word, Paul sent me this elegantly written tribute to the Benauds and to Richie in particular:

> It is a pity that the word 'celebrity' has become so debased that one would hesitate to apply it to a friend. Yet, in the world of cricket and in Australia's total population, Richie is a celebrity even though he has developed none of the many unpleasant characteristics that others have acquired in their climb to fame.
>
> Richie is without doubt the least complex famous person I know. He is as he sounds, as he appears to be, as he behaves. He does not deviate from a persona that was there from a very early age and has matured to the point of being legendary.
>
> He is entitled to think of himself as a person with a powerful influence on the game of cricket because he

has had that power for fifty years already. He has used it wisely, usually from behind the front line of publicity. Richie has such a natural ability to lead that he has no need to flaunt it. It is hard for anyone who is constantly in the public's eye to remain modest. Richie succeeds because his modesty is as inherent as his talents as a player and as an observer with opinions.

My wife and I were introduced to Richie and several of his team when he was visiting England as captain [sic] of the Australian side in the 1950s. He was a friend of a friend with whom he had stayed when playing in Nottingham. At that time we were living in Radlett, a village north of London, and our home quickly became a home from home to Richie and a few other Australians who appreciated the opportunity to drop out of sight of reporters and autograph hunters and the tour managers.

Since then we have met several times each year and have been regular guests in each other's homes. My wife and I have had years of opportunity to observe Daphne and Richie together. Their personalities are open to uncomplicated observation because neither of them is remotely devious.

They share a dedication to doing things as well as they possibly can be done. Perfection is their objective whether it is in choosing a restaurant or editing a manuscript or preparing for a broadcast. Daphne and Richie are not rich in celebrity terms, but they enjoy living the 'good life'. They travel internationally comfortably and efficiently, eat selectively, enjoy good wine, and dress immaculately and suitably for every occasion. They live all the time in character.

Richie, in particular, has been blessed with an encyclopaedic memory, and he loves to have it challenged. His fund of amusing and informative anecdotes is seemingly unlimited. His interpretation of all things 'cricket' is reliably wise and never arrogant.

Richie's modesty is loveable and we have experienced it many times.

Inevitably, he is recognised in restaurants which are either Australian or English for the English or in, say, Provence in France. We have observed his behaviour when his meal is interrupted by someone who has recognised him and wants to shake his hand and who wants to explain why. Invariably, Richie is tolerant, polite and a genuinely interested listener. The Benauds are ambassadors to the art of living inclusively and constructively with a foundation of optimism that is increasingly rare.

At just this time in my rather star-crossed quest, I severely injured my back—a prolapsed disk to be exact—and endured a couple of stints in hospital. On my return home, I found this message among the large backlog I was trying to clear: 'I have not received acknowledgement of my email and attachment of 04.03.11. Please confirm that you have received it.'

Perhaps it was because I was aching and irritable. Or maybe the elusiveness of Richie Benaud even at this early stage was subconsciously eating at my spirit and nerves. Whatever the reason, I replied with some annoyance. 'My record of replying appropriately and courteously to your correspondence,' I wrote, firmly ensconced on my high horse, 'was, I think, pretty good, and so you probably had no good reason to assume that I'd suddenly decided on a policy of curtly ignoring you, which I most certainly was not doing. Yours is one of the many emails and other correspondence that I'm presently struggling to catch up on.'

Paul's mild and reasonable reply—'I'm sorry you have been holed up for a few weeks. I was only asking for an acknowledgement that you had received my email; that's all, no reproof intended'—ended our correspondence on a regrettably sour note and it was entirely my fault. Like Rob Steen, like A. J. Symons in his quest for Baron Corvo and Ian Hamilton in his search for J. D. Salinger, I was beginning to wonder where all this was taking me and at what cost.

At that low point I called a halt and read Gideon Haigh's *On Warne*, and re-read C. L. R. James's *Beyond a Boundary* and Benaud's own *My Spin on Cricket*, *A Tale of Two Tests*, *Anything But...An Autobiography* and *Over But Not Out*. It occurred to me that I was quietly, without any fuss, giving up. Since that was not what I'd intended or wanted to do and was not in any case a characteristic reaction, I decided on a different tack, one that would fully honour Benaud's objection to biography but still afford a fair picture of the man and his achievements, as that engaging topic presented itself to me.

I would begin with a chapter, point–counterpoint, telling how it all started, and then go on to show how Richie Benaud aspired to and achieved mastery of his art, and how, in doing so, he changed the face of the game he loved, revolutionised the ways in which its innumerable charms, complexities and rituals were communicated, and became its welcoming voice and encouraging patron from rough-and-ready suburban ovals to the most famous Test arenas in the cricketing world. This would be anything but a biography: it would be a celebration.

2

RICHIE AND ME

My Part in His Career

'Sometimes an unlucky boy will drive
his cricket ball full in my face.'
DR SAMUEL JOHNSON, *The Rambler*, 1750

Richie Benaud and I go back many years. Like most Australian schoolboys in the early 1950s, I played backyard family cricket, but I also played Test matches. My opponent was a blond-headed ruffian called Tod, and we would take it in turns to be Australia or Australia's invariable opponent, England. In the 1951–52 season, however, the West Indies toured Australia and, in a revolutionary departure from what had been our normal practice, we decided on a series between Australia and the 'Windies', as our diligent study of the *Age*, the *Argus* and the *Sun News Pictorial* ('Daily at Dawn') had taught us to call them. As it was my turn to be Australia, Tod became John Goddard, the West Indies captain, and began to study his new list of players in the sports pages, as I settled into the more familiar role of Lindsay Hassett.

Representing and role-playing an entire team, however, was not our only trick. We were also selectors, and although it was our custom to follow the official selectors' example closely—'slavishly' might be more accurate—there were occasional and sensational departures. In this series I introduced one of them. In real life Richie Benaud made his Test debut on 25 January 1951 in the Fifth Test, and it was relatively inauspicious. He made 3 in the first innings and did not bowl, and 19 in the second. Hassett finally threw him the ball when nine West Indian second innings wickets were down, and he had champion batsman Everton Weekes dropped by wicketkeeper Gil Langley in his first over before going on to knock over tailender Alf Valentine for his first Test wicket, off the last ball of the match.

On our field of dreams, though, I selected Benaud—whom we youthfully mispronounced 'Benord'—for the Third Test. I don't now remember how I justified dropping leg-spinner Doug Ring, who took 6 for 80 in the real-life First Test and was a useful batsman—or maybe I was more innovative than I recall and played two leg-spinners in the same match.

Benaud didn't do much better in our game than did his other self. I had some idea of the grip for a leg-break, but I found it impossible to land the ball on the pitch—not that full tosses were necessarily a disadvantage in our contests because our pitch was a thinly gravelled back road, and when the slower ball hit the pebbled surface it could bounce vertically, or imitate violent leg-spin or off-spin regardless of how it had left the hand, or shoot only inches above the ground. Pace or medium-fast bowling was better because, although most of the deliveries skidded, they at least went straight.

When, in my Lindsay Hassett role, I made the bowling change that brought Richie Benaud on to bowl to Frank Worrell, even on our tatty strip—with the abandoned orchard at cover running through to mid-off and the boxthorn bushes spiky and treacherous at point, and my parents' new, half-fenced garden at midwicket—Tod and I sensed this was a dramatic moment. With my top four shirt buttons undone in careful imitation of my avatar, I became Benaud and bowled to Worrell/Tod, who promptly took me apart.

Benaud was removed from the attack soon after, but he stayed in my team, a daring selection, until real life caught up in the last days of January. No one but Tod and my father was aware of my prescience, and they didn't see it, needless to say, as at all prescient because 'Benno', as we had now learned to call him, didn't do much in my team and had a thin time of it in the actual Fifth Test. My old man reckoned he might come good, but they'd picked him too early. Still, something had begun, something between me and Richie—a kind of fateful preoccupation just falling short of obsession.

About a decade later our paths crossed again, briefly and ephemerally, but with the same tremor of possibility. In the early 1960s, I was one of that phalanx of Australian students—the best-known members among whom were Germaine Greer,

Robert Hughes and Clive James—who took off for Europe at the end of their undergraduate days. And it was in central Israel, somewhere near a place called Kfar Vitkin, that a few fortunate moments of hilltop transistor reception on Saturday, 8 July 1961 set a group of young Australian travellers on what seemed at the time a breathlessly daring path.

Kfar Vitkin as I remember it was, in 1961, a small kibbutz where we had been welcomed by the kibbuznik, roughly accommodated, and where we had done a few days' labouring in return for a roof, food and some mechanical attention to our VW Kombi. Nowadays it is apparently a moshav, or large township, and its inhabitants are known as moshavniks.

There, through the radio static, we learned that England had beaten Australia in the Third Test at Headingley, Leeds, by eight wickets. The series was squared and the Fourth Test at Old Trafford had suddenly taken on a critical importance. We decided to answer our country's call and make a breakneck attempt to get to Manchester by Wednesday, 26 July in time for the start of the Fourth Test the following day.

With the usual quota of mishaps, luck and eccentric though occasionally inspired decisions, we set out on Sunday, 9 July for Manchester, where the civic motto is *Concilio et Labore*—'By wisdom and effort'. Possibly short on wisdom, we nevertheless expended admirable effort and, with a cold English rain streaking the multicultural dust on our battered Kombi van, we rolled into town late on the afternoon of the 26th and found our way to Old Trafford.

If there were queues, we reasoned, we'd better join one and get some tickets; but I think we must have been too much haunted by memories of the MCG. There were no queues. No people. While we were standing there irresolute in gathering darkness, one solitary bloke emerged from the entrance gates and said, 'Evening, lads.' Instantly picking our accents when we greeted him, he joked about the coming game's foregone conclusion, as he saw it, and warned us about the weather.

'When you can just see the Derbyshire Hills in the misty distance from the Old Trafford ground,' he said, 'it's a sure sign of coming rain. When you can't see them at all, it *is* raining.' In short, the weather was looking dodgy, as the locals say; but, undaunted, we—Bob Dalgleish, Jim Evans, Ray Tynan and I—were intent on seeing every ball of the decisive Fourth Test. We were a dishevelled-looking group—travel-worn, weary, unshaven and, as we mentioned to our new friend, without shelter, having failed to find any affordable accommodation during the few hours we'd spent in Manchester since our arrival.

'Well,' he said, 'I can solve that one for you straight off.' He explained that he was an Old Trafford groundsman and knew his way around these parts. 'That building over there'—he pointed across the park to a long, low shed just visible in the thickening gloom—'that there's the Old Mancunian Cricket Club equipment store. It's full of matting you could sleep on, it's got electric light, and there's a lavatory and washbasin attached to the clubhouse next door. I'll open them up for you, and you can kip there tonight and stay on if you like, so long as no one twigs.'

Within minutes we were moving in. It was cold and, even with sleeping bags, moderately uncomfortable—the cricket matting looked inviting but was rock hard. In the rainy wind that seemed to blow most of the night, the whole structure rang with an orchestration of bumps, flappings and metallic creaks. But it was home, cost nothing, and was a few minutes' walk from the ground. We did not see our Good Samaritan again, but he must have kept quiet because nobody ever did twig and we stayed in uninterrupted residence until stumps were drawn for the last time, six days later.

When the flawlessly attired Richie Benaud and the similarly sartorial Peter May walked out for the toss, we might have been bristly and ragged around the edges, but we were well ensconced in good seats and ready to join the polite applause that greeted Benaud's winning call and his decision to bat. Peter May might have thought this a good toss to lose because the pitch was greenish, and the atmosphere damp and overcast. The Derbyshire Hills were still just visible, but every now and then they would begin to fade as if a curtain were being drawn across them, as indeed it was. The curtain was rain, but for the time being it did not fall on Old Trafford, and we settled in to watch every day and every ball of what would become one of the most famous Test matches in cricketing history.

Richie Benaud's persona, quite apart from the extraordinary feats of bowling and captaincy he produced at Old Trafford, was magnetic. There was something about him, even allowing for the bias of our youthful Aussie enthusiasm, that was captivating, impressive and somehow promising in the way that great characters—great people—are promising.

It is easy to say this kind of thing now, but even then Benaud seemed likely to grow beyond the confines of the field of play to become one of the important Australian figures of the twentieth century. It was in Benaud and his leadership and deeds that we saw the truth of what became an aphorism thereafter—and one not always spoken flippantly—that the captaincy of the Australian Test team is one step below the office of prime minister and occasionally, in the case of this or that prime minister, a step above.

Both teams had to do some shuffling—the English selectors to a side that had won handsomely at Leeds. Colin Cowdrey woke up on the morning of the match with the tonsillitis that had laid him up for the previous several days on the wane, but just a few experimental jogs showed him he would not last the five days and he withdrew. This brought the brilliant but out-of-form Ted Dexter and the quixotic Brian Close into serious consideration, while a Worcestershire seam bowler, the red-headed ('ranga', as the watching Australians would have said) and powerfully built Jack Flavell, came into the side in preference to Tony Lock.

As for the Australians: Colin McDonald had a wrist in plaster, so Bob Simpson moved up to open the innings with Bill Lawry, and Brian Booth, who had been batting beautifully in the lead-up games, made his Test debut at number six. Richie Benaud's injured shoulder, which had kept him out of the triumphant Second Test at Lord's where the Australians were led to victory by the vice-captain, Neil Harvey, was holding up without being fully healed. But despite the one enforced change, some of the Australians had something to prove. Peter Burge (5 and 0), Ken 'Slasher' Mackay (6 and 0), Simpson (2 and 3) and Benaud (a pair of ducks) all needed to put the Third Test behind them. Only Alan Davidson and Garth McKenzie, with eight first-innings wickets between them, had flown the flag.

Though we wore no adornments or colours, as became de rigueur years later, we were recognisably Australian, and we quickly became engaged in amiable chat, chiacking and argument with the people around us. Three venerable Lancastrians immediately in front of our seats were especially vocal, outlaying a provocative ball-for-ball knowledge of that disastrous Third Test and assailing us with dire predictions about what would happen in this one.

It was all very pleasant but, in the manner of such encounters, what happened on the ground endowed the friendliest of exchanges with a bit of edge, as, for example, when Lawry immediately and effortlessly off-drove Freddie Trueman—the destroyer of the previous Test—for 3 and, conversely, when Simpson's attempted leg-glance off Trueman came off the back of his bat and went through slips for 4. The groans and derision of our fellow onlookers had scarcely subsided when Simpson parried at the next ball outside the off stump and was caught by the wicketkeeper, John Murray. And so the famous Fourth Test at Old Trafford was underway.

I had learned the meaning of the word 'virtual' as a schoolboy when Neil Harvey, forced to come in early after the failure of an opening batsman, was called 'a virtual opener' by the commentators. This was what he now did, striding on to the cold and overcast oval with the score at 1 for not much, and the weather bleak and deteriorating and absolutely not the sort in which to be whacked by a fast bowler. Not that any of this seemed to influence Harvey. Although Lawry was sedate, scoring with quiet steadiness, that nose always over the ball, Harvey took to Brian Statham and Trueman, making most of the 14 runs Statham conceded in his first three overs and coping with Flavell's debut over, though not without the odd scare. Trueman, meanwhile, went for 29 in his opening six overs, and Australia's 50 came up in forty-six adventurous, sometimes heart-stopping minutes.

We were vocal in our approval of all this, having been badly set back by Simpson's early departure, prompting our Lancastrian acquaintances to turn round to us often with wry cautionary gestures or advice. When Harvey, who seemed well in control, was nicely caught at slip by Subba Row off Statham and the new batsman, Norm O'Neill, was almost bowled next ball, our friends' wryness and stereotypical dourness were leaning towards smugness.

Jack Flavell was one of those bowlers about whom the word 'bustling' is often used. The greenish wicket, and Flavell's strength and pace and air of impatient aggression, didn't impress Lawry, but O'Neill seemed thoroughly unsettled. Flavell hit him twice with successive balls, both times above or below the protection of batting pad or thigh pad. When O'Neill, obviously discomforted, resumed, he missed a pull shot and was hit fair and square in the groin. As O'Neill dropped to the ground doubled up in agony, an English voice observed above the orchestration of 'oohs' and 'aahs' circling the ground like a chant, 'Right in the balls.' For most of the grown men watching, and especially for those who had played cricket at any level at all, it was a wince-making, eye-watering moment.

There was a long delay, but when O'Neill finally faced up again, in one of the most courageous moments I have seen on a cricket ground, he went for exactly the same shot. This time it sped through midwicket, where it was supposed to go.

O'Neill, badly shaken, struggled on, getting an inside edge off Statham straight into his stomach but then hitting him for 4 before pausing to be sick just a few steps from the pitch after a sharp single. Bill Lawry, meanwhile, soldiered on, watching in dismay from the other end when O'Neill's day ended pretty much as it had proceeded—sensationally. Hit on the arm by a bouncer from Trueman, he overbalanced and flicked a bail off with his foot.

Lawry and the new batsman, Peter Burge, went to the lunch interval intact, and the morning's play, which had been thoroughly absorbing and given neither side a clear ascendancy, became the subject of much conversation, dispute and specula-tion over cold pork pies and warm beer. In a brief post-lunch flurry, Flavell bowled Burge, Brian Booth got off the mark, Lawry smashed Trueman with a hook and a drive, and then it rained—solidly and with grey determination. Over a few more beers and before abandoning Old Trafford for the day, our three Lancastrian friends wondered what adventures, good luck or consummate planning could have brought us to this ground and this match on this its first day…

As well they might. But that was another story.

The short answer was Richie Benaud. Only a matter of months earlier, under bright Queensland skies and over five extraordinary days of cricket, Benaud had joined Frank Worrell—with contributions from luck, benign fate and the exquisite skills of the two teams—in changing the face of Test cricket. Here was a figure of captivating importance, influence and quality. This Richie Benaud was worth travelling a long way to see.

That evening, following the early close of play as rain finally swept in over the Mersey, we went to a Chinese restaurant near the ground. There were only a couple of other diners and, in contrast to our awestruck, almost rude staring, they were clearly uninterested when Richie Benaud, Neil Harvey, Alan Davidson and 'Slasher' Mackay walked in and, once settled, began reviewing the state of play—which was 4 for 124, Lawry not out 64 and Booth not out 6. We could hear just about everything. When we left, we gave them a politely muted round of applause and some Australian vernacular encouragement and, to our surprise and delight, we shook hands all round.

3

TOMMY BENT, SIERAKOWSKI'S AND THE TIED TEST

The Penrith Boys

'I believe, looking back, that both games were connected, that
Manchester was part of a pattern, following the Brisbane game
in excitement and fluctuation and, at times, in courage.'
RICHIE BENAUD, *A Tale of Two Tests*

'The West Indies were well liked. Australians might have barely
acknowledged their own black population, denied them
the vote and broken up their families, but they saw nothing
incongruous about applauding a coloured cricket team.'
GIDEON HAIGH, *The Summer Game*

To fully understand and savour the magnetism and dramatic
presence of Richie Benaud as he led the Australian team into
that Ashes-deciding Test at Old Trafford in July 1961, we have to
leave, for the time being, Talbot Road, Brian Statham Way and
Warwick Road, Greater Manchester, and travel back about eight
months in time to late 1960 and seventeen thousand kilometres
south to Point Nepean Road in south-east Melbourne where,
on the hot afternoon of 14 December, people were gathering at
Sierakowski's Brighton Club Hotel.

This popular pub saw many historic gatherings before

inevitably succumbing to the combined forces of what governments inelegantly describe as infrastructure necessities—Point Nepean Road had become a broad highway to cope with the choke of traffic spawned by the sprawl of seaside suburbs—and commercial premises jostling for space and expansion as old Brighton gave way to brick veneer and a labyrinth of courts, cul-de-sacs, crescents and renovated, enlarged roads.

One of the more memorable of these occasions took place on 24 September 1966, when the St Kilda Football Club, in whose team the young Brian Sierakowski was an important defender and ruckman, won its first and still only VFL premiership. The triumphant St Kilda team gathered that evening at Sierakowski's for a raucous and lengthy celebration of their one-point victory. Supporters packed the bars and crowded the footpaths around the pub, and on the cool spring air floated ever more ragged and bleary versions of the Saints' club song.

Nearby, standing unmoved and high on his granite plinth in statuesque dignity, Sir Thomas Bent, a past mayor and luminary of Brighton, surveyed the scene with a stoic distaste which, had he been alive, would have been seen as unforgivably hypocritical because, despite his dynamism and energy in many social and political causes, 'he was [recognised as] a master of lobbying, log-rolling and obstructive tactics.' But neither his virtues nor his infamy mattered to the Saints' fans fifty-seven years and one week after 'Tommy' Bent's death, as they swarmed over his pedestal and statue, and left him proudly wrapped in a red, white and black St Kilda jumper.

Probably Sir Thomas Bent—'a formidable left-handed, round-arm fast bowler with the Coast Cricket Club,' according to the Australian Dictionary of Biography—would have been more interested in the similarly large gathering that took place at Sierakowski's on 14 December 1960. Every bar was packed. As the hot afternoon lengthened and the cold beer flowed, the ABC's cricket commentary boomed out from numerous speakers taking listeners to the 'Gabba, where Richie Benaud and Alan Davidson were leading a cavalier assault on the West Indies and seeking a victory which for most of the day had seemed improbable but was now in sight.

Generally speaking, and allowing for isolated exceptions, Test cricket in the 1950s had been stodgy and unadventurous, and had accordingly suffered a waning of interest in the Test-playing nations of that time. Australia lost the Ashes in 1953 and funereal over rates became the norm in 1954–55, with English bowlers especially culpable in stringing out the whole routine of walking back to the mark, pausing, pausing some more, then the run-up—the skip or hop, or the giant stride—and at last the delivery, the ball on its way.

In 1956, as if to put a final emphatic mark on cricket's 1950s decline, the English off-spinner Jim Laker took 19 for 90 in the Fourth Test at Old Trafford on a pitch that the former Australian opener Arthur Morris, writing in the *Daily Express*, judged to be 'not properly prepared for a match of this kind'. Benaud thought the pitch 'terrible' but, as the Australians recognised, its terrors did not prevent England from making 459 runs on it.

Towards the end of that fairly dismal cricketing decade there was much argument about the state of the game in cricket-playing nations, and many plans, adjustments and remedies were canvassed. In the Australian discussions, as the English biographer Charles Williams elaborates in his *Bradman: An Australian Hero*, the relationship between Don Bradman and Richie Benaud became crucial.

> It was not, in the true sense, friendship—the difference in age and temperament was too great for that. But Benaud recognised to the full Bradman's knowledge and experience, while Bradman for his part recognised Benaud's willingness, and ability, to engage in a cricket match with the same intensity as had Bradman himself. Furthermore, they had a shared objective...[By] the end of the 1950s cricket was in danger of losing its position as Australia's national game. Attendances... had fallen off badly—it was not unusual to see fewer than 10,000 spectators for a Test at Sydney or Melbourne. If the trend continued both Bradman and Benaud knew that cricket would wither and, at least in its traditional form, die.

In the West Indies and Australia, rejuvenation of the game and how it was viewed would be the subject of remarkably similar power struggles leading up to the 'Calypso summer' of 1960–61. As far as the West Indies were concerned, it was assumed that the board would reappoint the wicketkeeper-batsman Gerry Alexander as captain for the Australian tour. But the other candidate, Frank Worrell, had a powerful and articulate ally in C. L. R. James, whose *Beyond a Boundary* is one of the greatest and most celebrated cricket books ever written. As editor from 1958 of the *Nation*, the newspaper of the People's National Movement party, James set out, in his own words, 'to dislodge the mercantile-planter class from automatic domination of West Indies cricket'.

The dislodgement program was direct and unequivocal. The argument against Alexander left no room for ambiguity—one of James's pieces in the *Nation* was headlined 'Alexander Must Go'. His case for change was likewise direct and uncluttered: 'The best and most experienced captain should be captain—what has the shade of one's skin anything to do with it?'

The campaign failed to make Worrell captain for the English tour, but in the *Nation* of 4 March 1960, undaunted, James launched his Sunday punch: 'Frank Worrell is at the peak of his reputation not only as a cricketer but as a master of the game. Respect for him has never been higher in all his long and brilliant career.'

With what we can now see as extraordinary prescience, James argued that Australians wanted to see Worrell as captain. 'Thousands will come out on every ground to see an old friend leading the West Indies. In fact, I am able to say that if Worrell were captain and Constantine or George Headley manager or co-manager, the coming tour would be one of the greatest ever.'

Well, thousands did come out to see Worrell and his team—managed by Gerry Gomez, another inspired choice—and thousands farewelled them in Melbourne with one of the most extraordinary displays of public affection and admiration ever seen in that sport-obsessed city. As if it weren't triumph enough for Frank Worrell to have been the first black man to captain a West Indies team through a Test series, his predominantly black team had transfixed Australians across the country and had, without any missionary intent, struck a more or less inadvertent but nonetheless resounding blow at the White Australia policy.

Meanwhile, Richie Benaud had already risen to and thoroughly graced the position and title of Australia's Test cricket captain, but the journey, like Worrell's, had been circuitous and bumpy. Both he and Neil Harvey had been critical of Ian Johnson's captaincy during the 1956 Ashes-losing series: many of Johnson's tactical moves were regarded as either odd or frankly puzzling, and he antagonised or at least annoyed some players, Benaud among them, with his insistence that all players attend all lead-up games before the Tests began. Though both Benaud and Harvey were coming into consideration to succeed or replace Johnson, the Board of Control had strongly and consistently favoured Johnson, first over the charismatic Keith Miller—nominated in later years by Benaud as one of the five greatest Australian captains—and then over Harvey.

When Miller retired as the New South Wales captain, Benaud was expected to succeed him, but to everyone's surprise, including his own, Ian Craig was appointed. Craig went on to lead his team to victory in the Sheffield Shield competition, and subsequently captained the Australian Test team to New Zealand and South Africa. On the latter tour, in particular, his leadership was outstanding. Among other moves and decisions, he twice successfully enforced the follow-on, and he managed to keep Ian Meckiff and Jim Burke, whose bowling actions were coming under suspicion, away from the eyes of any umpires likely to be difficult.

His own batting form, however, was poor. It may not have mattered—aside from Bill Lawry in 1971, historically Australian captains have not often been summarily abandoned—but during that South African tour the press, including Keith Miller, began to canvass the possibility of Craig's being dropped. Neil Harvey and Peter Burge were Craig's fellow selectors on the tour, and Harvey, speaking for himself and Burge, pointed out firmly that Australian teams did not drop captains on tour and while he had any say in the matter this practice would not be changing in South Africa.

The final Test, at Port Elizabeth, was in Benaud's view a triumphant one both for Craig as captain and Harvey as his deputy. But this description could have been applied to the whole tour and certainly to Benaud's own experience of having taken thirty-odd Test wickets and made two centuries. Despite his outstanding form, on returning home he felt convinced that in the imminent Ashes Series, Neil Harvey should again be Craig's vice-captain, Craig's miserable tour with the bat notwithstanding.

Benaud himself was entertaining no thoughts whatsoever about the captaincy. But it wouldn't be so easy. Craig, seriously ill with hepatitis, was forced to drop out of cricket for the season, and Benaud became captain of the New South Wales team. Harvey meanwhile had moved to Sydney and would play for New South Wales under Benaud. As Benaud conceded wryly, despite his great pleasure in having Neil Harvey as a team mate, the whole situation had suddenly become extremely complicated.

On 26 November 1958, the Australian selectors seemed to have boldly resolved these complications. Benaud was named captain for the First Test in Brisbane, and Harvey was to be his deputy. Benaud was uncharacteristically cautious about the honour. He was disappointed that Harvey had once again been overlooked and acutely aware that the whole process had been influenced by changes in luck.

He also suspected that his appointment was not universally approved of, and that some officials who were full of praise and congratulations in public were less enthusiastic in private. So, although he admitted to being pleased by the appointment, he remained wary of Janus-faced supporters. It was not the first time and it would not be the last that Benaud harboured doubts about the genuineness and capability of some of cricket's administrators.

As opposing leaders Frank Worrell and Richie Benaud would form one of those friendships that seem inevitable. It was not just the many things they had in common and, more particularly, their shared experience of coming to the cricket captaincy of their nations along a road made bumpy by administrators; it was also a bond, an alignment of personalities, that each instantly recognised though neither might have consciously considered.

'All who saw Worrell,' said the cricket columnist Vaneisa Baksh in a speech marking the fiftieth anniversary of Worrell's appointment as captain, 'remark on the beauty and grace of his movements, the polish of his manners, the elegance of his dress and deportment, and his almost languid ease in any social circumstance.' Allowing for the different cultural environments into which Worrell and Benaud moved as their status changed, the Australian experience being more easily navigated than the varying and often conflicting demands of the island nations, this description might also apply to Benaud.

'Sir Frank Worrell,' Baksh concluded, 'was nothing short of a work of art.' Likewise in the days of his pomp, Richie Benaud was handsome, tidily but not obsessively neat, composed but with a sudden coiled-spring athleticism, socially gracious and engaging, on the field a deceptively casual exterior masking a commanding, calculating and relentless spirit.

And so, with their different backgrounds, their shared experience of not being precisely the men their cricket bosses desired and their mutual temperamental inclination to make the game of Test cricket once again enjoyable for all concerned, Frank Worrell and Richie Benaud strode on to the 'Gabba for the toss on 9 December 1960.

Worrell, winning that toss, chose to bat, and the first day of what would become one of the most important Test matches was launched with a cameo performance by Alan Davidson, who removed Conrad Hunte, caught by Benaud, and Cammie Smith and Rohan Kanhai, both caught behind by Wally Grout. When Davidson had begun his fluid, loping accelerating run to deliver the first ball of the match, there were five men in the slips and no third man, on the theory that the highly talented but adventurous West Indian top order would have to 'nick one' before they were settled.

With 65 on the board, Garfield Sobers arrived, slashed at and missed a couple early then, in Benaud's words, 'took over the whole game'. For just under three hours, partnered mostly by Worrell, he flayed the Australian bowling in a masterly batting performance. As the Australian opening batsman Colin McDonald recalled it fifty years later at a reunion of many of the players from that Test: 'On the first day we wondered if we'd ever win a match, because Sobers crucified us. It was brilliant batting. He made one of the greatest hundreds ever; I haven't seen a better one.'

At the same gathering, the Australian off-spinner, Lindsay Kline, chatted with Sobers and recalled that innings: 'I said to Garry..."That wonderful innings you played, that 130 was fantastic." And he said, "Lindsay, it was 132." So it must have been pretty special to him, because he made a lot of hundreds.'

Although Benaud knew exactly where he was going to pitch each ball and mostly succeeded in hitting the spot exactly, he later confessed he had no idea where Sobers was going to hit it. As Benaud remembered the innings, Sobers 'drove Davidson, cut him and pulled him. He "hoicked" ['Slasher'] Mackay from a good length past square like a rocket. Kline and [Ian] Meckiff were unable to contain him and he took my bowling as a personal affront.' It was a rare experience for Benaud, who conceded 90 runs in his twenty-four overs. Even worse was having to watch helplessly—but admiringly—as Sobers dismantled the Australian attack and humbled its strike force.

With Sobers' spectacular century at its heart, the West Indies' innings finished on a daunting 453, only to be eclipsed by Australia's reply of 505, with Norm O'Neill contributing a stunning 181. The West Indian second innings faltered to 284, Worrell topscoring with 65, and Australia began a run chase of 233 early on the morning of the fifth day.

Benaud recalled arriving at the ground on that final day and noticing something had changed. It was a bit like that moment in *The Bridge on the River Kwai* when, on the morning they are due to blow up the bridge, Shears (William Holden), Major Warden (Jack Hawkins) and Lieutenant Joyce (Geoffrey Horne) wake to an eerie silence. The river that had been on the previous night rushing, frothy and swirling is in the first light of day almost silent; it has gone down in the night, they realise, exposing their explosives and wiring.

In his River Kwai moment, Benaud walked through the gate at the 'Gabba for that last, incredible day and realised, vaguely at first, that things looked different. White clover flowers speck-led the grass: the ground had not been mowed that morning. Quickly finding the curator, Benaud asked him to get the mowers out, but showers earlier had soaked the ground and by the time the Australian captain made his request it was too late to act. Ruefully reflecting that perhaps he should get out and mow the grass himself, Benaud decided that it probably wouldn't matter as Australia needed only a little more than 200 to win. A few hours later, Australia were 6 for 92 and Wes Hall had four of the wickets.

Hall had been a towering presence throughout the game, but on that last day he was a giant. Alan Davidson, no stranger to the ills and woes of fast bowlers, marvelled not only at Hall's fine bowling but also at his physical endurance. 'Wes Hall bowled magnificently, when you consider that he had new boots that he hadn't been wearing, and he had these giant blisters on the bottom of his feet. He ended up putting this great slab of sticking plaster across the soles of his feet after he'd cut the blisters off. Really, it was just raw flesh, and he kept pouring in and bowling his heart out. That was one of the most sensational things I've ever seen on a cricket field. He must have been going through agony.'

But sensation was to be their element that day and at 6 for 92 most of the sensational possibilities seemed to be in West Indian hands. Benaud was still in, however, and Davidson had joined him, and they, and their team mates, knew this match had an undercurrent just as sensational as anything that had already happened on that remarkable field in the morning.

That undercurrent, as Benaud remembered it, began before the match started at the usual team meeting, which Sir Donald

Bradman, the chairman of selectors, had asked if he might attend. Although visits of this kind from selectors in the twenty-first century are unremarkable, in the climate and routines of 1960s cricket administration this was an extraordinary request. Bradman's short speech was equally out of the ordinary.

In a brief but pointed address, Bradman encouraged the players to anticipate a great cricketing year in 1960–61. By setting their sights on attractive, attacking cricket, they had it in their power, he said, to make the Australia–West Indies series live up to the promise that was already exciting the country. The incentive could not have been clearer: aggression and good cricket would be rewarded, and tactics and behaviour that short-changed the people coming through the turnstiles would be frowned upon. It was a clear reference and reaction to the stodge of the 1950s.

This, to say the least, remarkable statement stunned the listening players. This was leadership from the administration, the lack of which Benaud had remarked on several times earlier and would do so again as the years passed.

No doubt every player present recognised the artlessly subversive nature of Bradman's statement, but Benaud saw it as a historical moment. He understood immediately that Bradman was reacting, above all, to the slump in cricket's profile and fortunes in the 1950s, but at the same time sensing and under-standing the spirit of the age in which the venerable game of cricket could be renewed—the Age of Aquarius, the dawning of the 1960s. Although he would not, under any circumstances, have put it in those terms himself, Bradman, with Benaud's enthusiastic support, was inviting Australian cricket to 'let the sunshine in'.

The convergence in the West Indies 1960–61 tour of four distinct, reforming and reinvigorating forces is almost uncanny: C. L. R. James, with his determined and courageous domestic championing of Frank Worrell and his confident prediction of Australian excitement at a Worrell-led West Indies tour to Australia; Worrell himself, a daring, canny leader and the first black man to captain a West Indies team; Sir Donald Bradman, with his intuition that an opportune turning point had been reached when everything about Test cricket might be rejuvenated; and Richie Benaud, who recognised and captured the 1960s' mood and spirit that would sweep cricket up in its momentum, along with so much else. More than half a century later, with Test cricket under siege from Twenty20 and in decline in several countries, players, administrators, writers, sports journalists and theorists might learn from the charismatic 1960s—though they'll have to find twenty-first-century equivalents of James, Worrell, Benaud and Bradman, potent ingredients in a volatile and creative mix.

When, for the second time in that match, Bradman visited the players, Benaud and Davidson were having a cup of tea before resuming the chase in the last session, undaunted by the 141 runs still needed and the 6 wickets down. As newspapers all over the country would later report, Bradman asked Benaud whether he was going for a win or a draw. When Benaud assured him they would be going for a win, Bradman replied, his poker face betrayed by a twinkle in the eye, that he was 'very pleased' to hear it.

Back in the middle, Davidson and Benaud launched a furious attack that brought Australia to within 7 runs of the target but also close to disaster.

'I went in at 5 for 57 in the second dig,' Davidson recalled fifty years later, 'and it wasn't that I thought we had the game sewn up. I'd spoken to Richie with two overs to go. It was tip and run, and I said, "We don't have to do anything silly, just make sure that I'm down there to face Wes," because I reckoned Wes would bounce me once—well, that was either a 4 or a 6, and we only wanted 7. Richie played the first three or four off Sobers and then hit it straight to Joe Solomon and took off. If I'd been Usain Bolt I wouldn't have made my ground.'

In came Wally Grout, whose extreme nervousness had not settled at all when, on the point of walking out of the dressing room, he couldn't find his gloves. 'They were in the top of his pads and of course the moment he stood up, they went back in against his thighs and so he couldn't find them.' As for the rest of the team: 'When I got back inside,' Davidson said, 'I wouldn't have said they were the calmest in the world.'

In retrospect, however, Davidson was generous about how events unfolded. 'It was impulse,' he reflected. 'We had been playing that sort of cricket. We'd been hitting it and taking off, and we [forced]…some wild returns resulting in a few overthrows, and the pressure was building. That's where Frank

Worrell did a terrific job in pacifying some of the more excitable players in the West Indian side.'

The West Indians were not the only excitable ones. With one eight-ball over to go and 6 runs needed for a win, Grout took Hall's first ball in the stomach painfully, and Benaud ran as the ball fell at the batsman's feet. Grout, rubbing the instant bruise, staggered home at the other end.

As he prepared to face the next ball, Benaud was not expecting Hall to pitch short, later explaining that Worrell had earnestly and emphatically ordered Hall not to bowl any bouncers. In Worrell's position Benaud would have given exactly the same order, and so he convinced himself that Hall would not risk bowling short. But a bumper it was, fast, dangerous, hookable. So he hooked. It was a typical Benaud reaction, fully in line with the assurance he had given Bradman. But this time it didn't work and the wicketkeeper, Gerry Alexander, let out a victory cry as he caught him off his gloves.

With Benaud out, Ian Meckiff joined Grout, played the third ball securely and tried to hit the fourth out of the ground. 'I was just trying to get bat on ball. It was a bit short and I just had a slog at it. Wesley even said [during the reunion] when he looked at it again he was surprised how good the shot was. I didn't tell him how I felt—it was just shut-the-eyes-and-slog.'

But his slog, however agricultural, could have won the game and must have taken Benaud back to his River Kwai moment that morning, when he had noticed the thick, clover-sprinkled grass. Hours later, as Meckiff's big hit pulled up short of the fence, Colin McDonald echoed his captain's observation with a good deal more anguish: 'The curator had neglected to cut the grass that day, so the ball that Meckiff hit, a certain boundary, got into the long grass not far from the fence and just stopped. It was long grass—a sure 4—but it didn't make it, and the third run was a run-out. That third run would have been enough to win the match.'

In the dressing room, 'Slasher' Mackay had forbidden anyone to move. As McDonald remembered it, 'He wouldn't let us move from our seats for fear of divine intervention. He was fairly superstitious. Nobody was saying very much.' Only half an hour earlier Lindsay Kline had been assured by McDonald that he probably wouldn't have to bat, but no one could have foreseen the manner of Grout's exit. It was a miracle, the subject of dramatic still photographs all over the cricketing world, and a sequence played and replayed endlessly for years to come. Conrad Hunte, down at fine leg, was close to the boundary when he gathered in Meckiff's 'certain boundary' as it plodded into the thick grass, and then with one smooth uncoiling action landed the ball in Gerry Alexander's gloves over the top of the stumps.

Recalling it with characteristic precision, Benaud noted that it was not to one side or the other, not right, not left but directly over the top. Grout was racing but still failed to beat the 'miracle' throw.

This superhuman coup brought Kline to the middle, but not before, like Grout earlier, he 'lost' his gloves—he'd been sitting on them. As he walked past Frank Worrell on his way to the wicket, Worrell said, 'I wouldn't be in your shoes for all the tea in China,' adding, 'You look a bit pale.' Kline felt distinctly pale, but his mind was clear about their strategy. 'We're going to run on this ball no matter where it goes.'

Kline took guard and waited for Hall to start his run. 'Wes bowled it on the stumps, I got the bat to it, and it went round the corner to square leg, where Joe Solomon picked it up and threw the stumps down side-on.'

Strictly speaking, Peter Lashley should have done the fielding. 'I was at square leg,' Lashley recalled, 'and Solomon at midwicket. It was coming to my right hand, which was my throwing hand, and his left hand, not his throwing hand. I was the likely person to pick the ball up, but he'd just knocked down the stumps to run out Davidson, and he said, "Move, move, move!" So I stopped, he swooped, picked the ball up and hit the stumps again. Had I picked the ball up there would have been no Tied Test!'

And that was that. It was all over—except that not everyone was sure where things stood.

Ian Meckiff wasn't even thinking of a tie. 'I thought we needed 233 to win, so 232 didn't mean anything to me at that stage.' Lindsay Kline, conversely, was sure one run would win it: 'I'm running for a win and Ian's running for a tie. But I can understand it, we didn't have electronic scoreboards or anything, flashing up "one run to win" or anything like that. I thought he knew, and I thought I knew.'

The West Indian wicketkeeper, Gerry Alexander, was totally

confused. 'We were coming off the field a little bit concerned. We knew we hadn't won, but at the same time we knew we hadn't lost. It was a bit difficult at the time to put things in perspective.'

When Colin McDonald asked a disconsolate Meckiff why he was looking 'so downcast', Meckiff said, 'We've lost, haven't we?' To his amazement McDonald replied, 'No, it's a tie.' 'Then, after that,' Meckiff said, reliving the euphoria of an extraordinary moment, 'it became a big celebration.'

For Alan Davidson, 'The most amazing part was that at the end of the day's play, when everyone realised what it was, Frank got his team together and Richie got his, and [in] the dining room were these long tables, and we had a West Indian and an Australian, a West Indian and an Australian, all the way around that table. The conversation and the laughing—we spoke about every possible thing, there were some talking about family, there were others talking about the tours they'd just come from—it was an amazing thing that after five days of battle, here we were sitting and laughing and chatting...

'We played our hearts out against each other. If I meet a West Indian who played in that series now, we don't shake hands, we just go into a bear hug. When you think about that, and that it's fifty years on, it's an incredible feeling.'

Even cricket history's second tie—Australia versus India at the M. A. Chidambaram Stadium, Chennai (formerly Madras), in September 1986—could not dull the sheen of this famous game. Neil Harvey's fear was that 'once we got two ties, everybody would forget about the first one.' But, to his surprise, this did not happen: partly because, though the two games shared the same extraordinary result, they were very different in character and atmosphere.

Of the second tie, Kapil Dev recalled, 'It got quite tense out in the middle and we did not take kindly to some of the Australian tactics. There was a lot of gamesmanship going on…' The cricket historian Norman Giller saw in the Chennai match 'none of the sportsmanship and adventurous spirit that made the Brisbane Test…cricket at its very best'.

Harvey, echoing Bradman, saw the bigger picture: 'I think it's because it was such a great series. The Tied Test was remembered as such because it was the series that got the crowds back to cricket.' Colin McDonald, with a suggestion of his captain's sense of history, was more assured. 'I thought, well, there's never been a better cricket match and the fact that it's a tie means that it's going to be there forever. And it has been. There was another tie played, but it doesn't have the same recall of our Tied Test match. When you talk about the Tied Test, it's usually ours.'

There are many ways in which this famous match was the product, the artistic creation, of the two captains. It was not that Worrell and Benaud knew each other well, or could look back over a long acquaintance, although Benaud had watched with interest and some disbelief the machinations surrounding the West Indian captaincy in 1955, when C. L. R. James was championing Worrell and the West Indian cricket administration was sedulously ignoring him.

When the West Indian team arrived in Australia for the

1960–61 tour, Benaud had greeted Worrell at the airport and they chatted briefly before Worrell headed for the plane to Perth, where the tour was to begin. But when Benaud called out his good wishes for the coming summer of cricket, Worrell turned and, retracing a few steps, assured Benaud that whatever happened they would have some fun. It was a perceptive remark. Australian cricket was about to be shaken to its core in the best possible way, the kind of shaking that gets rid of dust and the clinging shreds of a disposable past. Neither Worrell nor Benaud could predict as much with any assurance, but in that brief, amiable encounter at the airport, both felt inexplicably a sense of possibility and potential.

Benaud's description of this moment in his *A Tale of Two Tests* is spare, tellingly observant—Worrell stopping, turning, coming back to acknowledge the pleasantry—without frills or gesturing, yet with a kind of poignancy, an ability to intimate without gaucherie or self-consciousness the experience of two men feeling the beginnings of a profound bond, like George Orwell's reaction to his meeting with the Italian militiaman in *Homage to Catalonia*: 'I hardly know why, but I have seldom seen…any man…to whom I have taken such an immediate liking.' Benaud and Worrell were glimpsing, in a way they themselves hardly comprehended, a future in which they would both play stylish and magisterial parts.

By the beginning of the 1960s, with an Ashes victory still fresh in the national sporting memory, Australians already knew that Benaud was not just an outstanding cricketer and leader, but also a presence—a striking figure, assured yet properly self-deprecatory; articulate, socially adept, intelligent and modern; daring and innovative. As C. L. R. James saw him at 'the speech-making after the last Test [of the 1960–61 tour,] Benaud was fluent, with carefully chosen phrases, full of affection and respect for Frank Worrell and the West Indians—and not forgetting his own team; definitely a man of feeling, not ashamed or wary of it, but a man seeing the whole of his world and steadily.'

In Worrell, towards whom James was understandably somewhat biased, he saw 'a glimpse of what brought a quarter of a million inhabitants of Melbourne into the streets to say goodbye to the West Indian cricketers, a spontaneous gesture and in cricket without precedent, one people speaking to another'. In this grand and unique conversation Richie Benaud had played his crucial and highly individual part.

At Sierakowski's on that evening of 14 December when the first Test tie gradually became clear to crowds in the bars, there was amazement, puzzled jubilation, a kind of undifferentiated joy—we hadn't won, yet somehow everyone recognised the singular nature of the moment. As Bradman explained to a disheartened Benaud, 'This is the best thing that could possibly have happened for cricket.' To Davidson he said, 'Don't be disappointed, Alan. Today you've made history.'

And that was the view gradually adopted by the jovial crowd in Sierakowski's. We had been part of a historic game, even if it had happened way up north and reached us only on the radio—the television coverage, black and white, was confined to the

Brisbane metropolitan area and the radio voice was not Alan McGilvray's. Convinced the game was lost, the much-admired commentator had left to catch an early plane.

Outside in the warm dusk, Sir Thomas Bent was his usual, unruffled, stony self. He'd seen plenty of sporting moments, but this one, and Richie Benaud's magnificent role in it, was special because although Brighton, Victoria, was where Tommy Bent had lived most of his life and where he made his not wholly spotless reputation, his birthplace, like Benaud's, was the western Sydney suburb of Penrith.

4

ISRAEL TO OLD TRAFFORD

Bowling into Freddy's Footmarks

'Go together, / You precious winners all; your exultation /
Partake to every one.' WILLIAM SHAKESPEARE, *The Winter's Tale*

'The Brisbane tie had much to do with our win at Manchester...
the tie and the West Indian series established a pattern of play
for our Australian side.' RICHIE BENAUD, *A Tale of Two Tests*

Like the Australian team, we can now return our attention
to the early stages of the Old Trafford Test with the amazing
experiences of the Tied Test fresh in our minds. At Old Trafford
occasions for cheering had been fairly sparse. There was Bill
Lawry's defiance on the first day and his gradual mastery of
the attack, and there was Norm O'Neill's courage in the face
of fast-man Flavell's bruising assault, which had the young
batsman doubled up in the worst kind of pain after being hit in
the worst place and then crouching nauseated at the edge of the
pitch after a quick single. And there was Peter Burge's sudden
attack on Trueman just before lunch, cutting him through an

aggressive field for 4, then hooking the bouncer that predictably followed in a flash to the boundary, very nearly taking the ducking Statham's head with it.

Whatever Richie Benaud and his senior players had planned during their Chinese meal, it wasn't evident when on the following morning Lawry and Brian Booth walked out to resume the Australian innings. Against the odds, and despite local opinion to be heard outside the ground and around the turnstiles, rain didn't seem likely. The morning was fine and dry, if dull, while as the afternoon wore on a burst of sun across the ground was apparently such an un-Mancunian phenomenon that the crowd applauded. Perhaps they appeased Jupiter Pluvius, or 'Huey' as Australians say, because it did not rain again for the rest of the match.

Our Lancastrian mates were among the doomsayers confidently predicting meteorological Armageddon, and we failed to distract them with our story about meeting Richie Benaud and his team mates in the restaurant. So there was nothing for it but to have an early pint or two and discuss the weather and its discontents until day two began on time, and Lawry and Booth took the score up to 150 with a steady stream of runs off Statham and Flavell. The drying breeze played across the bright grass, an etching light seeming eerily not of the sun glowed in the fluffy clouds, and the solid northerners settled into a rapt, murmurous continuo rising and falling according to the pock-pock or ringing crack of bat on ball.

But then Lawry, who had scarcely looked like being

vulnerable, was beaten by Statham cutting the ball surprisingly into the left-hander's pads and catching him squarely LBW. Mackay joined Booth, and they both prodded and missed and took painful blows on hands and hips, though in between these uncertainties Booth played some cracking shots. So unpredictably did the contest waver between bat and ball that our verbal scuffles with the three elderly Lancastrians became a resigned, pleasant stand-off. Nothing either side could say would, for the moment, be apposite; it all depended on what happened, ball by ball, out in the middle.

Booth got some revenge for O'Neill's suffering on the previous day by hammering Flavell out of the attack, but Statham toiled on, tempting Mackay not to 'slash' but to leg glance so finely that he deflected the ball straight to the keeper, John Murray, and walked. Replacing Flavell, Ted Dexter tied Alan Davidson in knots and the all-conquering Statham from the other end had Booth caught by Close, giving him his first 5-for against an Australian side in a home Test.

When Richie Benaud strode to the middle, it was as if we could now all admit—we Aussies anyway, although English applause was strong and generous for the captain—that this was really what we had been waiting for. Richie had arrived. He would see us through.

It was not that Benaud had had much of a tour so far. Three for 15 and 36 not out in the drawn First Test at Birmingham was a fair start, but then injury forced him out of the Lord's Test, in which Neil Harvey, Test captain for what would be the only

71

time in his distinguished career, led the side to victory. Benaud returned for the Third Test at Leeds, but his unreadiness for combat was perhaps demonstrated by his uncharacteristically ordinary performance—1 for 86 and 1 for 22 with the ball, and a pair with the bat.

He was not alone, however. In the first innings of the Headingley Test, Trueman took 5 for 16 and Australia's last eight batsmen contributed a total of 50 runs in five overs. In the second innings Australia managed to eclipse even this dismal effort, losing the last eight batsmen for 21. This time Trueman took 6 wickets for 4, including Harvey, O'Neill, Simpson, Mackay and Benaud without conceding a run. Australia was comprehensively beaten, thus making it possible for the Fourth Test at Manchester to assume its pre-emptive mystique.

Indifferent form notwithstanding, Benaud had about him an aura that even the grey, unforgiving skies and sharp, muscle-tightening breezes of the northern hemisphere did not diminish. Some visiting players, and among them sun-loving Australians, seemed to shrink into their sweaters, to tuck down into raised shirt collars like snails backing into their shells, when the watery light faded, the grass chilled and the whack of a crisply driven ball catching the bottom joints of tensed fingers set nerve ends jangling all the way up the arm. But Benaud, compact in a sweater or, in mellow weather, with shirt unbuttoned to the navel (or so it seemed), always looked as if he belonged.

Athletic, handsome, somehow effortlessly in charge—even through those periods during some classy opponent's murderous innings when neither he nor the team was the slightest bit in charge—Benaud commanded respect, even awe; or, in the words of the 1980s Australian fast bowler Geoff Lawson, 'a touch of reverence'. 'Even when his side was in trouble,' Ian Chappell recalled, 'he would stand in the gully, arms folded, looking very calm. After a while he would snap his fingers and everyone thought this would be the move. And it would be.'

From his early days in first-class cricket the gully became Benaud's terrain but, as a brilliant young, inexperienced fieldsman, he did not always exhibit the calm that Chappell admired. Prowling his territory on the first day of the Third Test against South Africa in Sydney in January 1953 and, as he himself conceded, inching ever closer to the bat and the catch that must come, he stopped a John Waite square cut with his mouth. With smashed-up gums, dentures in pieces and a split top lip, he was helped from the field while pressing a towel to his bloodied face, but somehow the characteristic Benaud panache ensured that he still looked the part. This was how you should look when you 'wore one' close to the bat. And what you should do was return, patched up, to the field of play on the third day, which is what he did. His only blemish in a game he could have been excused for abandoning amid the scars and the wounds was a twenty-two-minute duck, but 2 for 21 with the ball in a resounding victory was some compensation for the blood, the stitches and the dental outrage.

Benaud was already something of a favourite in England. His sportsmanship, his polished appearance, his articulate, considered statements to the media as captain and, above all, his attitude to the game—his determination to attack, to take risks, to entertain—appealed to even the most dour and biased Pom. So far, however, Richie Benaud had been almost in the background of the 1961 tour. The injury—a torn tendon in his right shoulder, sustained in an early game at Worcester—caused him at times great pain and nagged away at his bowling action even after he returned.

Most of those who watched him stride to the wicket that day at Old Trafford would have known about, possibly even seen footage of, the last few overs of the Tied Test only a few months earlier in Brisbane. But this time, striking presence though he was, Benaud brought only anticlimax.

With Grout gone and number eleven McKenzie his partner, Benaud had made 2 when he played all round a ball from Dexter and lost his leg stump. Australia's total of 190 looked even worse at stumps when, despite some fine bowling from Benaud, conceding 5 runs in five overs, Peter May was untroubled on 90, Brian Close—playing Test cricket against Australia for the first time in ten years—was sticking around nervously, and England with seven men still in the shed were on 187. Wherever they sat down to dinner that evening—we returned in hope to the Chinese restaurant but alas they didn't show—Benaud and his men had much to talk about.

As far as England were concerned, the third day got off to a rollicking start, with May cautious in the shadows of a century while Close hit Benaud back over his head for 6, smashed a full toss from McKenzie for 4, then edged Davidson through slips for another boundary. In the time Close scored 20, May made 5—and then got out for 95 touching a ball on off stump which went too wide for Grout but bounced up and out of the keeper's gloves into the safe grasp of Simpson. Close, who had been looking entirely belligerent and moderately in charge, then suddenly departed LBW to McKenzie. With new batsmen Ken Barrington and wicketkeeper John Murray at the crease, England were a mere 22 in front and staggering. Benaud's decision to call for the new ball after Close had taken to him proved a canny one which realigned the game yet again. And the sun shone and the day warmed.

Barrington, a cricketer's cricketer, was much admired both as player and man by Benaud, among others. He had been known in his youthful days as a bit of a lad. On England's 1955–56 tour of Pakistan he led five team mates in 'kidnapping' the Pakistani umpire, Idris Begh, and pouring a bucket of water over him in mock protest at his bad decisions. Having forsaken the big hitting for which he had been known in his youth, Barrington had developed a fortress-like defence and could be a painfully slow scorer. In one game on that tour of Pakistan he took four hours to make 43, pinned down by the Pakistani paceman Fazal Mahmood. Five hundred and eighty-six runs at 39.06—the second best performance on the tour—apparently could not erase Barrington's bucket episode and it would be four years before he was called up again. But all that was behind him at Old Trafford when, having replaced his captain at the crease and been joined by Murray, he settled in to rejuvenate the English response—which he duly did, first with Murray, and then with David Allen, both of whom grew in confidence as he unflappably chaperoned them from over to over.

As Barrington went about the business of resurrecting the innings—instilling increasing confidence in Murray and then, when Murray suddenly shrank into his shell and nudged a catch behind, nursing Allen through early innings nerves and hesitancy—a low breath of excitement and anticipation animated the crowd. It seemed they understood that dramatic events were imminent and might be stymied by too much enthusiasm. This was the tension that gripped the third and fourth days of the match, which were quieter than the extraordinary dramas of the last day, because it was a time for probing, defending and calculating. One tactical mistake by either captain could have a disproportionate effect on the final result and therefore on the destiny of the Ashes.

Barrington, as the senior partner, proceeded at plodding pace and Allen followed suit whenever he had to take strike. Around the ground a steady, derisive slow clapping eventually broke out, as if the crowd were lamenting the loss of an opportunity to grab the game by the throat. And then, abruptly, despite some magnificent tight bowling by Davidson, Barrington did just that. He and Allen put on 30 in fifteen minutes. Our three Lancastrians had a pint each, raided their sandwiches before the tea interval and snatched glances at us in which triumph was denied by uncertainty.

Benaud's attempt to break the unlikely growing partnership with a leg-spin barrage, which he and Simpson delivered, failed. Barrington smoothly reached 50, England passed 300 and Allen, who had not long before made his maiden century for Nottingham, hit boundaries like a seasoned Test batsman. Benaud's nine overs went for 35 and the partnership had reached the mid-eighties when Allen mis-hit and the ball, designed for leg, ballooned out to the on side. It was a mark of both the Australians' eagerness and their growing frustration that Booth and Davidson almost collided going for the catch. But Booth juggled it and held on, and Allen was gone in time for tea when the score was 7 for 361.

'In t' box seat now, lads,' was the exultant view of our three chums when play resumed after tea. They were right. With an accomplished batsman to guide and shelter the tail, England could contemplate a lead of 200 in the first innings. But Benaud turned to Simpson who, aided by some utterly inexplicable impatience in the batsmen—as if they needed to rush to a score before stumps—made his captain's very good decision look like sheer genius by taking 3 wickets for 2 off twenty-two balls. And so, with about an hour and a half to go, Australia embarked on their second innings 177 behind.

At the end of that day, Simpson and Lawry had moved Australia 63 runs closer. Subba Row dropped a speeding chance from Lawry in the slips and the same batsman was astonished to see a ball from off-spinner Allen—bowling for the first time in the match—fizz out of Trueman's footmarks and deviate so much that it passed the wicketkeeper and was fielded by first slip. Benaud, watching from the balcony, observed this with great interest.

Soon after, the umpires lifted the bails, Simpson and Lawry walked off undefeated and, on that Saturday evening, the teams, in those gentler, slower times, went to their day of rest, which would consist variously of sleeping in, playing golf, socialising and, for most at some stage of the day, even if only quite briefly, a session in the nets.

We went to our rest too, though rest was not an accurate description of what one experienced on the cricket matting. Still, we weren't complaining and on Sunday morning, armed with a swag of weekend papers, we took over a table at a small local café and whiled away a few hours reading various experts' versions of the three days of cricket we'd just witnessed. The proprietor, who served our satisfyingly greasy breakfast and kept the bad coffee coming, was pleased we'd chosen his establishment for our Sunday-morning relaxation. Well, he would be, wouldn't he, but apart from his perception of the commercial advantages of having four hearty eaters on the premises he quickly picked us as Australians with whom he could maintain a running, chiack-ing conversation as he navigated around his customers, most of whom were only too willing to join in.

All accounts agreed that Lawry and Simpson had looked impressive as they ensured they would start again on Monday morning, but some of the scribes noted a momentum established in past encounters that seemed to be—ought to be—a burden for the Australians. It was often pointed out that Manchester was not a favoured venue for Australia—before 1961 they had played seventeen Ashes Tests at Old Trafford, winning only twice—and it was also famous for being the only ground where Don Bradman failed to score a Test century. Many believed, moreover, that Benaud's dodgy shoulder was obviously still a problem and he might not see out the next two days.

Meanwhile, the Australian captain was also thinking. Supposing Lawry and Simpson carried on their partnership, and the other Australian batsmen prospered, England would be chasing a fair total on a fifth-day wicket. What if he—Benaud—bowled his leg-breaks into the visible rough stirred up by the pounding boots of Statham, Flavell and especially Trueman? The wicket itself was holding up well. It was only really suffering along the line of footmarks made by Freddie Trueman's follow-through. The fast bowler's scuffing, dragging and pounding boots had torn into the surface outside the line of the stumps at both ends.

But apart from these musings, which he recorded later in his account of the Test, Benaud didn't explicitly address the interesting nature of the wicket and the poised state of the game. It was, after all, a rest day. Golf, sightseeing, letter writing and relaxing were the preferred options, but all the players and especially their captain were aware of an underlying tension, an impatience to get going on day four because only then could they exercise some influence on the Ashes.

On the morning of the fourth day, Benaud—acting on a

captain's hunch—arranged to have breakfast with Norm O'Neill who, he felt, without being able clearly to explain why, could hold the key to success. He knew that the young and brilliant batsman was still smarting from his physically and mentally bruising first innings encounter with Statham and, especially, Flavell. Just about everything had gone wrong for him, and the manner of his dismissal set the seal on an appearance O'Neill himself regarded as a complete disaster.

But all batsmen, no matter how capable, have the odd bad day—even Garfield Sobers, despite the destruction he had wrought on that first day at the 'Gabba only a few months earlier. Benaud reminded O'Neill that he had all the attributes to turn the tables on the English pace attack, then went off to a brief strategy meeting with Neil Harvey, who agreed that the plan should be to attack or, if things went wrong, to try to keep England under such pressure as would convince them to play for a draw.

An expected massive crowd, a sell-out, prompted us to forsake our cricket matting beds early and claim our usual spot. When the players arrived, the excitement around the packed ground—its gates closed, the outer jam-packed—was palpable. Play started on time under a cloudy but bright sky and in fine, crisp conditions. Predictably, May began with Statham but then brought on his spinner, Allen, at the other end bowling…where else but into the footmarks outside the left-handed Lawry's off stump.

Bill Lawry and Bob Simpson would become one of the great opening partnerships in Australian Test cricket history, and on that fourth day of the Fourth Test at Old Trafford they gave a glimpse of things to come. Both were good players of spin and though they scarcely scored against Allen they nevertheless played him comfortably, and when he at last overpitched Lawry cover-drove him for 4 to reach 50, his second for the match. The hundred partnership came up in 130 minutes and Simpson celebrated by straight-driving Flavell for 4 to reach 50 in his turn. But then he was out, brilliantly caught behind by Murray.

Harvey arrived at the wicket to play an extraordinary innings in which crashing boundaries through covers and down the ground were mixed with edges—one of which flew straight into and out of Close's hands—and complete misses, especially to Trueman, whose exasperation was evident to even the most distant member of the crowd.

Lawry completed a splendid century but was out immediately afterwards. O'Neill, having promised Benaud at breakfast that he would get among the runs, made a scintillating 50 but fell to Statham, whose second spell with the still-new ball was outstanding. O'Neill remarked of the ball that dismissed him: 'Brian is the greatest. He bowled me a couple moving in. The next one was pitched in exactly the same spot, but it went the other way.' Murray, giving the wicketkeeper's view, said, 'It was a beauty, moving away just enough to find the edge of the bat.' Statham said, 'It was straight.'

Australia began the fifth and last day of this utterly enigmatic match—a blue-skied, warm first day of August—on 6 for 268, leading by 154. It was not sufficient, but characteristically

Benaud was not interested in a draw, which conceivably could have been achieved if the batsmen had shut up shop, so Mackay and Davidson, two left-handers, started cautiously but had every intention of forcing the pace.

Allen opened the bowling, pitching immediately into the footmarks, and Mackay, having dealt imperturbably with two of these, was nicely caught by Close in the gully off the next one. Benaud joined Davidson, and it seemed that these two great all-rounders would now nail the game. But Benaud's very ordinary tour with the bat continued when, on the back foot instead of going forward, he was LBW to the dangerous Allen. Three wickets had fallen for 2 runs. 'Difficult to win from here!' someone said in the dressing room.

Grout was quickly gone trying to hit the ball into the next county and, with Allen having taken 3 for 0 off fifteen balls, the young McKenzie joined Davidson. The lead was 157, a figure which our Lancastrian trio rightly judged to be not nearly enough—and they told us so, emphatically, unequivocally and often.

They hadn't, however, bargained on Davidson. Nobody outside the Australian dressing room had. Even irrepressible supporters like us, brimming with antipodean optimism, didn't expect too much. But Davidson was about to give us one of those never-fading cricket memories and McKenzie was going to play much more than a bit part.

As Davidson remembered the start of that last-wicket stand, 'We had lost 3 for 1 in the first three overs in the morning, and...

Graham came out to bat. I am the seasoned Test international and he is in the embryo of his Test career. The amazing part about him was he was so relaxed. He was sort of half-whistling as he came out, he was so calm. I told him, "Righto, mate. It's up to us, just play straight. And we'll see what happens." The funny part is I remember stories being told and written in books that I was getting instructions from Richie from the dressing-room balcony. The truth is, I am short-sighted, so I could not even see the total on the scoreboard, the balcony was just a blur to me.'

May brought on Close, a potentially good decision in Benaud's view because the off-spinner's loop combined with modest turn might cause McKenzie problems. Close was a useful change bowler, sometimes a partnership breaker, but inconsistent and wayward. He bowled a succession of full tosses and McKenzie, looking as if he was marvelling at how easy this Test-match caper was, hit three boundaries.

Davidson then took to the previously unplayable Allen, whose nine overs had yielded just 2 runs. 'I had played six or seven maidens in a row because I did not want Graham facing Allen [but when Allen was recalled to the attack, replacing Close] I thought this might be my opportunity...Everything I hit came right from the middle.'

First he off-drove him for 6, then drove him through covers along the ground all the way for 4. Allen dropped shorter and Davidson smashed him off the back foot for another bullet-like 4. Mixing them up, Allen gave the next one a lot of air and Davidson planted it into the terraces or, as he described it: 'the last shot in that over, I hit…over mid-off and it was such a sweet hit and if not for the brick wall the ball would have landed in the railway yard.' For his part, Mackay was 'amazed the ball didn't burst'.

For Benaud it was a historic moment. 'I shall never forget the sight of that ball soaring in the air, higher and higher, until it smashed into the railway wall behind the despairing glance of long off.' It was at this point that one of our Lancastrians turned around irritably as we rose out of our seats cheering and clapping and said, 'Be quiet, lads, and watch cricket.'

From Allen's point of view, the story was slightly different, although his narrative amounted to the same brick wall in the end. With some regret he noted how expertly Davidson had farmed the strike to protect McKenzie, who faced only three or four balls from the spinner.

'Davidson made sure he took my end every over I bowled that morning. Also, the fact that our fast bowlers were trying to attack McKenzie at the other end never allowed me to bowl against him. As it happened, I bowled nearly eight to nine maidens that morning. Before I started my tenth over May asked me to attack Davidson, to flight the ball and mix it up with changes of pace. Davidson took the opportunity to hit two powerful sixes over cover and a couple of boundaries. Immediately May replaced me with the fast bowlers.'

This was a critical failure of nerve which the Australian contingent in the crowd, especially the four of us, greeted with relief and surprise because, despite the onslaught, Allen's off-spin would have undone McKenzie before very long. Davidson rampaged on to 50 while the 50 partnership took only thirty-nine chaotic minutes, with McKenzie, as if inspired by his partner, starting to claim his own sections of the boundary.

The crowd, from members to groundlings, seethed with tension and anticipation as Davidson carted Trueman all around the ground, and McKenzie played and missed, snicked, drove and cut capably for fours and twos. At last, when the partnership had reached 98, Flavell, replacing a psychologically bruised Trueman, bowled McKenzie and the innings was over.

England needed 256 at about 4 runs an over and they had 230 minutes to get them but, because their chase began before lunch, they would have to make three new starts: one to begin the innings, one after lunch and again after tea. Benaud was optimistic, calculating that a run-a-minute task compounded by the footmarks ought to be beyond England. Davidson too was upbeat. When he returned to the dressing room at the end of the Australian innings—the not-out batsman—he said, as he took off his pads, 'We'll do these jokers, Rich.'

Reportedly, as the various scribes chatted in the press box between the innings, Frank Worrell observed that the runs could be made if England were prepared to lose, meaning that May and his men would have to take risks and wear the consequences. More gloomily, John Woodcock of *The Times* suggested that England might lose three or four wickets in a resolute chase 'then come to grief against Richie'. The commentator and writer Jim Swanton predicted a failed run chase ending in a draw.

Down among the crowd, our local mates were gloomy and thought a draw was England's best chance, but even they, in their depths, agreed that the stage seemed to be set for heroic and remarkable deeds. Like Worrell, many felt that May and his men could win if they dared, and that they should at least go down swinging. 'That's what the Aussies would do,' said one of the Lancastrians, grimacing as if stung by his own treachery. Or the Australians could ride their luck and create a famous victory. Either way, it would require every player to hold his nerve and perform beyond his best, and there would have to be someone— an Australian bowler or an English batsman—to impose his will on the game, the way sports champions seem able to do, and dictate the unfolding of events.

As it turned out, two heroes emerged in the last innings of that extraordinary Test match—and one of them was Richie Benaud. The other hero—the one who was first on to the stage in this classic last innings of a classic Test match—was 'Lord' Ted Dexter. Dexter usually batted at number six, but he came to the wicket when the brisk opening partnership of Geoff Pullar and Subba Row ended with Pullar being caught at midwicket. Despite the anxiety which Dexter's magnificent aggression immediately engendered in us—two cracking off-drives for 4 off Davidson to begin with—it seemed as if such an adventurous approach could not last. But last it did. Dexter produced one of the greatest Test match short innings. My three friends and I agree that, of our many wonderful memories of that great experience at Old Trafford, Dexter's laser-beam drives and fizzing or delicate or caressing cuts—he produced them all at will—were among the most vivid and durable.

Benaud—following Davidson, who bowled eleven consecutive overs after lunch, and McKenzie, who was savaged by Dexter and quickly removed—bowled beautifully, but Dexter was indomitable. The hundred partnership arrived in seventy-nine minutes and the score sped to 150 in 123 minutes after Dexter hit Mackay into the terraces. Our Lancastrians were spending as much time turning round to us as they were watching the game, and our attempts to look bravely confident were weakening by the minute.

Dexter seemed unstoppable and bound for a brilliant, match-winning century. Recognising this, Benaud had a brief tactical discussion with his vice-captain and then the whole team. In order to do so on that chilly, overcast, thoroughly Mancunian afternoon, he called for drinks. He later explained that his odd request—certainly mystifying to the by no means warmly basking onlookers, including us—was the only way he could talk to all his team mates and quickly plan the next moves, a plan which Dexter's brutal onslaught had made urgent. What he realised, and what he told Harvey and the team, was that the match couldn't be saved: it would have to be won. A mighty effort was called for by bowlers and in the field.

Just after the 150 came up and Dexter had hit that big 6 off Mackay, he took a quick single to keep the strike. The run turned out to be one of those moments that so often occur in sport: some equilibrium was infinitesimally disturbed, though no one could possibly have sensed that this had happened. The stolen single brought a watchful Dexter up against Benaud, who bowled five successive tight, scoreless deliveries.

As Dexter recalled it, he was 'waiting for Richie to drop one short and I went for the cut against a ball that bounced a bit, was too close to me, and I nicked it. You have to give Richie good marks for going around the wicket. The reason he did that was not because he thought he could bowl us out but to stem the tide of the runs. Bowling leg-spin outside the leg stump is a famous way of drying up runs for the right-hander.'

That sixth ball may certainly have bounced a bit higher than Dexter expected, but it was a good one and a brave one nevertheless. He walked off to a standing ovation in which the Australian players joined. So did the Australian onlookers. It remains one of the finest innings I have seen in many years of cricket watching—attacking, bold, exquisitely executed, a small gem—'small' only in the sense that it didn't blossom into the century that seemed so inevitable and was so thoroughly deserved.

It was nerve-wracking enough being on the field as the minutes passed and the English batsmen sparred at Benaud as if he was, according to the cliché, bowling hand grenades, but among the rest of the Australian squad, watching nervously and spellbound from the dressing room, 'no one was allowed to move from his seat, and Ron Gaunt was barred from taking photographs [because] every time he appeared with a camera while play was in progress something disastrous happened.'

It was by no means all over, yet it was as if Benaud's conquest of Dexter had somehow doomed the rest. As Dexter himself said, 'The wheels fell off immediately after my exit.' Coming around the wicket into the footmarks outside the right-hander's leg stump, Benaud removed May, 'bowled behind his legs', as Dexter—who had scarcely got his pads off—described it, and skittled Subba Row to go into tea having taken 4 wickets for 9 runs off nineteen balls.

After tea Benaud continued to attack variously around and over the wicket, accounting for Murray and Allen, both brilliantly caught in slips by Simpson. One of these catches—another inerasable memory—was snatched when the ball had actually flown past him. A mopping-up operation by Davidson to clean-bowl Statham brought this stunning Test match to an end.

Benaud had bowled thirty-two consecutive overs to take 6 for 71 in the last fifteen. According to Ashley Mallet, a close friend of Neil Harvey, towards the end of Benaud's marathon stint Harvey was urging him to bring on Davidson and apply the coup de grâce, but Benaud was intent on a seventh wicket. Finally, in Mallet's version of events, in exasperation Harvey fielded a ball in the covers and returned it so wildly it nearly ran away for 4 overthrows. Benaud stared at him in disbelief. Harvey, a brilliant fieldsman and a deadly throw, stared back and said, 'Now will you bring Davo on?' Or so the story goes.

Davidson's own recollection was pointed. 'Benaud had bowled for something like three overs into the footmarks [trying] to get rid of Statham, but it took me about three balls. I bowled a fast leg-break off the foothold to dismiss Brian to win the match.'

So ended a Test match that would take its place in history and remain for all the players on both sides one of the greatest they ever played in. There were many highlights and turning points—Dexter's coruscating innings, Lawry's gnarly century, Davidson's onslaught, Allen's off-spin, O'Neill's courage—but, as the light faded over Old Trafford after stumps on that last day and we trailed out with the crowd, some bemused, some joyous, some, like our North Country friends, philosophical, there was really only one name dominating memories, discussions and arguments: Richie Benaud, bowling into the footmarks and stealing the game.

It was, as Rob Steen wrote, 'Richie's finest hour as player, leader and adventurer.' How prescient was John Woodcock's 'We will lose three or four chasing them and then come to grief against Richie.'

Scapegoating began almost as the last wicket fell and was so fierce, in the murderous way at which the English press is so adept and eager, that Benaud joked that perhaps the English team had not merely lost a Test match but had threatened to overthrow the monarchy. Easily the main target, however, was Brian Close. He would scarcely recover from the drubbing he received from the predatory reporters, but he had one sturdy, though perhaps unlooked for, supporter in Richie Benaud, who rated the attack on Close as grossly unjust.

Conceding that the Englishman certainly could have done better, Benaud nevertheless speculated that Close's ill-fated attempt to hit his side out of trouble and towards victory had been under instructions. What looked like Close's suicidal addiction to sweeping the ball with the spin had been, in Benaud's view, the right tactic. It was just that he didn't connect often enough or well enough. It was not only Dexter who had him worried, Benaud confided later. Close could turn games very quickly and, with better execution and a slice of luck, could have turned this one.

Benaud was similarly open-minded and generous about the result, suggesting that luck had not run with the English players. Although he did not mention his opposite number, Peter May, his views on captaincy stand as an implied critique of how the English managed the tense fluctuations of the Old Trafford Test, during which the momentum changed so often. It was a matter of recognising, grabbing and capitalising on whatever break came along, he thought, and of attacking, of having the courage to take risks when safety looked more attractive and would certainly be protective of individual reputations.

Benaud was firmly convinced in retrospect that the results at the 'Gabba, in the Tied Test, and at Old Trafford, in the Ashes-saving Fourth Test, came about because the Australians—bowlers, batsmen, fieldsmen alike—thought only of attacking, no matter how dire the situation seemed at a given moment. Benaud's own example, of course, as a leader, tactician and especially as a bowler who risked everything to exploit the conditions, was crucial and inspiring.

Among the Australians, after the match there was triumphant incredulity. 'I don't think I have ever seen such emotions,'

Alan Davidson said. 'We were laughing but tears were running down our faces. It was an incredible thing. It was a bit like the Tied Test…That was a perfect Test match. I was lucky enough to play in the Tied Test. But I have always rated the Manchester Test as the second-best.'

Ray Lindwall called it the 'best game' he had ever seen outside the Tied Test of 1960. Benaud made the same immediate comparison as Lindwall and Davidson. The sequence of the two Tests was in his view as extraordinary as the amazing events and result in each. But to have a match like the Tied Test precede by only a few months the credulity-testing triumph at Old Trafford would have strained even the most willing reader's patience if it had been written as fiction or a script. To recognise them as two of the greatest Test matches ever played was Boys' Own stuff—but it was true. And there was more, a deeper structure, to the apparently serendipitous: as Benaud noted, 'The Brisbane tie had much to do with our win at Manchester…the tie and the West Indian series established a pattern of play for our Australian side.'

PART
II

5

CAPTAINCY AND GRACE IN DEFEAT

Vizzy and Richie in Kanpur

'Captaincy is 90 per cent luck and 10 per cent skill.
But don't try it without that 10 per cent.' RICHIE BENAUD

Kanpur in Uttar Pradesh was the stamping ground of an extraordinary member of the Indian cricket community whose path would cross Richie Benaud's. It was also the venue—Green Park Stadium—for a famous Test match between India and Australia, and a wonderful display of sportsmanship by the Australian captain. With all its network of coincidences, luck and random encounters, it went like this...

Born on 28 December 1905, Lieutenant Colonel Sir Vijay Ananda Gajapathi Raju, second son of Pusapati Vijayarama Gajapathi Raju, was seventeen when, on the death of his father, he assumed the title of Maharajkumar of Vizianagram and succeeded to the family estates in Varanasi. Vizzy, as he came to be known, was a young man of great promise, having attended Mayo College in Ajmer—styled by the 1st Earl of Lytton, Viceroy of India, as an 'Indian Eton' and the place for the 'education of India's young rulers and nobles'—and then on to Haileybury and Imperial Service College in England. Though an ordinary scholar, Vizzy was an excellent tennis player and a fine cricketer and, on his return to India, aged only twenty-one, he formed his own cricket team and provided it with a ground and facilities in his salubrious and well-endowed palace precinct.

In *Anything But...An Autobiography*, Richie Benaud notes that Monday, 6 October 1930, the day of his birth in Penrith, New South Wales, was dominated by a sensational news item from Beauvais, France, describing the crash and destruction on the preceding Sunday of the British airship R101. Other news that did not, however, make it to Penrith for the Benauds' big day reported that Mahatma Gandhi's civil-disobedience campaign, known as the Salt March, was continuing to produce widespread social unrest throughout India, despite Gandhi's arrest on 5 May.

In a curious and roundabout way—perhaps a characteristically Indian way—this far-off, utterly symbolic event, forcing the cancellation of a planned English tour of India, set in motion a chain of quite fateful repercussions. Cometh the hour, cometh the man: Vizzy stepped into the breach with a team of his own to tour India and Ceylon. Pre-dating the seductive India Premier League by some eighty years, Vizzy convinced two international stars, England's Jack Hobbs and Herbert Sutcliffe, to play for his side.

The tour was a great success, with Hobbs and Sutcliffe both scoring heavily. They were no doubt unburdened by anxiety or nervousness because neither of them regarded the matches they played in as anything more than exhibition games, and they duly used their extraordinary batting talents to provide the expected entertainment. *Wisden* reported the matches as having less than first-class status, but later cricket statisticians took a different view, so that both players have two versions of their career statistics, one that recognises the feats of Vizzy's tour (500-odd runs and two centuries to each of them) and one that does not.

But Vizzy's self-indulgence would have a much bigger effect on cricket history. In order to join Vizzy's Indian tour, Sutcliffe had declined selection in the official English team to tour South Africa in 1930–31 because the two fixtures clashed. He was replaced by Andy Sandham, who had partnered Hobbs in many county opening stands and was a capable, recognised batsman. Sandham started well against Western Province before disaster struck. As *Wisden* bemoaned it, 'The absence of the famous Yorkshireman [Sutcliffe] became a very serious matter when Andy Sandham, after scoring 72 and 6 in the opening games, met with a motor accident which prevented him from playing any more during the whole course of the tour.'

South Africa won the First Test by 28 runs, and the ensuing four matches were drawn. The England captain was Percy Chapman—characterised by his biographer, David Lemmon, as a tremendously popular figure on and off the field. As Martin Chandler notes, reviewing Lemmon's biography, Chapman was, above all, 'a stylish and aggressive left-handed batsman and, in his time, a fieldsman who had no equal'. He was 'no sort of a disciplinarian and no great tactician, but he somehow managed to bring out the best in all he had dealings with, and he was renowned for living life to the full'.

Returning from South Africa as a 1–0 loser, however, Chapman was doomed, and he was replaced as captain by Douglas Jardine. If the English selectors had consciously set out to choose the opposite of the gregarious, easy-going, somewhat bibulous Chapman, they could not have fixed on a more precise antithesis than the aloof, bloodless Jardine.

And so, at the end of a string of events obscurely initiated by the upheavals following Gandhi's Salt March, Jardine took the English team to Australia for the 1932–33 series, where he masterminded the infamous Bodyline or 'leg-theory' attack which, designed expressly to nullify Donald Bradman, almost brought the series to a standstill during the Adelaide Test, looked likely to provoke a diplomatic incident and has festered in the Australian consciousness ever since. It is doubtful if Vizzy would have noticed, but his initiative in securing the services of Hobbs and in particular Sutcliffe was the butterfly effect that created the conditions for Bodyline and the storm of controversy that proceeded from it.

Storm is a good metaphor for Vizzy. It was in his incarnation as a turbulence that he forced himself into Richie Benaud's gaze following a famous Indian victory at Green Park Stadium, Kanpur.

Indian cricket has come a long way since then, but that Test remains in the minds and imaginations of many of that nation's cricket buffs because it was the first time India had beaten Australia in a home Test match. India won the toss, batted and made 152. Benaud (4 for 63) and Davidson (5 for 31) were in commanding form, but Australia's reply of 219, of which Benaud made 7, scarcely capitalised on the efforts of the bowlers. India's second innings of 291 (Contractor 74, Kenny 51, Davidson 7 for 93) set Australia 225 for victory; apart from McDonald (34) and Harvey (25), the batsmen didn't give a yelp (O'Neill 5, Davidson 8, Mackay 0, Benaud 0), and India won by 119.

It was a famous victory, and Benaud acknowledged it handsomely and with great style, going onto the ground to shake Indian skipper Gulabrai Ramchand's hand as soon as the game was won, and then lining up his players to applaud the victors and following them into their dressing room to congratulate them personally. This sportsmanship was celebrated by none other than Vizzy, whose rambunctious personality exploded in his report of the match in Kanpur's main newspaper, *Dainik Jagran*.

As Benaud dryly notes in *Over But Not Out*, Vizzy saluted the victory 'a touch flamboyantly', comparing it honourably with signal events of the year 1959. Since these included, among much else, Russia's Lunar 2 crashing on the moon, Fidel Castro coming to power in Cuba, the invention of the microchip, and Alaska and Hawaii becoming the forty-ninth and fiftieth members of the United States, it was a long bow Vizzy was drawing, but in his enthusiasm no claim was too extravagant. The Australians, he wrote, had forsaken their 'ethereal heights' and tasted 'the dust' of defeat. They had done so, he conceded, with matchless grace and spirit.

In the Northern Indian *Patrika*—an Allahabad newspaper—Vizzy told a different story, slating what he purported to have seen as the Australians' lack of sportsmanship and recommending that they never return to India. It was this article, drawn to his attention by a friend who was an Indian journalist, which prompted Benaud to throw Vizzy out of the Australian dressing room when he burst in full of bonhomie just before the start of the Bombay Test.

As Benaud recalled the encounter, Vizzy's hail-fellow-well-met greeting quickly turned to bluster. He was invited to apologise and to explain how such an offensive—and inaccurate—article could have come about, but he insisted that someone else, and certainly someone junior, had written it. Attempting to turn the attack back on Benaud, Vizzy announced that his good name and reputation had been impugned. As Benaud pointed out later, he behaved as if he owned the cricket club—which, given his wealth, he might well have done. Warming to his theme as he recounted the incident, Benaud wondered if Vizzy owned Bombay.

There was no reason why Benaud should have been better versed in Vizzy's mercurial ways. He refers correctly to Vizzy's title and position as the Maharajkumar of Vizianagram who, in 1936, had captained an Indian Test team in England, but Benaud is rightly not concerned with further detail. It's just that Vizzy's behaviour would have made more sense to him—although it would have appeared no more justified—had he known something of the back story, and Vizzy's odd, oblique contribution to the Bodyline crisis and his flamboyant, self-regarding presence in the labyrinthine world of Indian cricket administration.

In truth, Vizzy's captaincy in England was fraught from the very start. He was perceived to have gained his position by influence and lobbying, there were acrimonious team splits, and Vizzy himself behaved more like a tourist than a team captain. According to the legendary Indian cricketer Vijay Merchant, Vizzy was rarely seen on the playing grounds of England with the Indian team, spending more of his time attending sessions of the House of Commons and the House of Lords, and socialising with blue-blooded men and women of the United Kingdom, and his players noted and resented his absenteeism.

Not surprisingly, some comprehensive thrashings ensued. The team lost both the First and Third Tests by nine wickets but managed a draw in the Second after England's only innings was declared at 8 for 571. As captain, Vizzy achieved the dubious distinction of sending Lala Amarnath home before the Test series had begun. Merchant was not alone in his view that

> Amarnath was by far the best player—with bat and ball—in the early stages of the unhappy Indian tour…

Furthermore, Amarnath knew he was the best player and, having waited, padded up, during an unusually big partnership in the match against Minor Counties at Lord's, he was infuriated to be told that other batsmen would be promoted ahead of him. He swore at the captain and tour treasurer, and was sensationally sent home. The team's subsequent failures, a commission of inquiry, and history as written by people with a more egalitarian world-view than Vizzy's have all combined to exonerate Amarnath. But it meant a twelve-year gap between his third Test and his fourth.

Vizzy was roundly criticised in the inquiry—the January 1937 Beaumont Committee—that followed the tour. His captaincy was rated as 'disastrous'. More damningly, the report found that Vizzy 'did not understand field placings or bowling changes and never maintained any regular batting order'. His quixotic team selections meant that 'good players remained idle for weeks.' The report found Amarnath not guilty of any of the charges alleged by Vizzy and completely exonerated him. As for Vizzy, he never played for India again.

Not surprisingly, Vizzy maintained a low profile thereafter for almost two decades. He made a comeback as a cricket administrator and was the president of the Board of Control for Cricket in India from 1954 to 1957. As the vice-president of the BCCI in 1952 he had, bizarrely, given his history, played a role in bringing back Lala Amarnath to the national captaincy.

From the 1948–49 series against the West Indies, Vizzy, re-established as a senior figure in cricket administration and commentary, became a well-known radio voice and was the guest commentator for the BBC during the Indian tour of England in 1959. He was not a particularly good caller. According to a colleague, when Vizzy had just finished describing how he had hunted tigers—tiger hunting was one of his passions—the champion West Indian batsman Rohan Kanhai responded, 'Really? I thought you just left a transistor radio on when you were commentating and bored them to death.'

Lala Amarnath emerged from the exile and strife into which his clashes with Vizzy had plunged him and became, among other things, chairman of selectors. Once again, Vizzy had exerted the butterfly effect. Amarnath, alternately pressured and supported by Vizzy, used his position on the selection committee to insist—against all opposition and repeated arguments to the contrary—on a shock selection of a spinner for the Kanpur Test.

To Richie Benaud and his team, Amarnath's selection of Jasu Patel came entirely 'out of the blue'. They had never heard of Patel but soon saw the reason for Amarnath's insistence. In India's 119-run victory Patel took 14 wickets.

Not for the first time and certainly not for the last, Richie Benaud seemed to stand almost nonchalantly, as if by preordainment, at one of cricket history's intersections. Improbably strung together by the unpredictable decisions and ventures of the quixotic Vizianagram, a series of events as distant and different from each other as Gandhi's Salt March and Jardine's Bodyline had, in their obscure ways, brought Australian Test cricket to its first loss on Indian soil, and thereby evoked from the imperturbable Benaud one of the most gracious and generous gestures of sportsmanship in defeat in the annals of the game.

6

WANDERERS TOUR OF 1976
Benaud and 'Baboo'

'As far as criticism is concerned, we don't resent that
unless it is absolutely biased, as it is in most cases.'
B. J. VORSTER, prime minister of South Africa, 1966–78

Richie Benaud was commentating for BBC television in 1968
during the Fifth Ashes Test played at the Oval. England won by
226 runs, squaring the series but leaving Australia in charge of
the urn until the MCC's next antipodean tour. The match was
an important one for the South African-born Basil D'Oliveira,
whose first innings of 158 put him in line for selection in the
MCC touring party to South Africa. Amid much argument
and counter-argument, D'Oliveira, a British citizen but a Cape
Coloured by South African standards, was not selected in the
side, and it seemed that a volatile situation had been defused.

An injury to Tom Cartwright, however, led the selectors

to include D'Oliveira, and the South African prime minister, Balthazar Johannes Vorster, then declared that this would be unacceptable under his country's apartheid policy. Denis Howell, the British minister for sport, announced in a parliamentary statement that the 'MCC has informed the [South African] government that the team to tour South Africa will be chosen on merit…If any player chosen were to be rejected by the host country, then…the projected tour would be abandoned.'

When, in 1975, Benaud was invited to be manager of a private cricket tour of South Africa, he instinctively refused partly because, having personally witnessed the trials, strain and confrontations endured by managers of cricket teams, he had resolved never to accept a managerial role. But apartheid and its horrors were constantly in the news; it was hard to look away and, for cricketers and cricket lovers generally, the sad D'Oliveira affair lay damningly in the recent past.

Vorster, in a provocative speech, had said, 'We are not prepared to receive a team thrust upon us by people whose interests are not in the game, but to gain certain political objectives which they do not even attempt to hide,' which meant that a team including D'Oliveira would not play in South Africa. As Michael Melford observed in *Wisden*,

> A dignified speech of regret might have done something
> to heal the wounds, but Mr Vorster broke the eighty-
> year-old links between English and South African
> cricket in a speech for internal political consumption—

in crude and boorish words, as the *Daily Mail* editorial
put it—and with a harshness which can have won him
little sympathy outside his own party.

On 24 September 1968, the MCC committee had formally
cancelled the projected tour of South Africa. Conscious of all
this in 1975, and of the continuing complexity and seriousness
of apartheid, Benaud began to pay attention. And, when the
appointment with the touring Wanderers club seemed a possibility, he engaged in a broad range of discussions, trying to see
past the dogged entrenchment and prejudice.

The proposition that South Africa was blameless and that
there was no problem he regarded as 'rubbish'. On the other
hand, he found the unrelieved gloom of the critics unenlighten-
ing. The management position with the Wanderers offered the
opportunity for him to do it his way, to go and see for himself
and make up his own mind. And so, with some trepidation but
a clear idea of the non-negotiable terms that would govern his
agreement, he accepted.

The Wanderers who finally assembled to make the trip
under Richie Benaud's managerial eye were Greg Chappell
(captain, Australian), Ian Chappell (Australian), Mike
Denness (a Scottish-born English player), Phil Edmonds (a
Zambian-born Englishman), Gary Gilmour (Australian), Alan
Hurst (Australian), Martin Kent (Australian), Dennis Lillee
(Australian), Ashley Mallett (Australian), John Morrison (New
Zealander), John Shepherd (West Indian), Bob Taylor (English),

Glenn Turner (New Zealander), Derek Underwood (English) and Max Walker (Australian).

The South African Invitation XI was captained by Eddie Barlow. His team was drawn from Clive Rice, Vintcent van der Bijl, Hylton Ackerman, Howard Bergins, Henry Fotheringham, Jack Heron, Denys Hobson, Lee Irvine, Peter Kirsten, Douglas Neilson, Gavin Pfuhl, Graeme Pollock, Anthony Smith, Barry Richards and Lorrie Wilmot. Coloured players selected in accordance with Benaud's stipulation that they must be represented were Abdullatief Barnes, Winston Carelse, Ismail Ebrahim, Devdas Govindjee, David Jacobs and Farouk Timol.

The tour took place during March and early April, and the International Wanderers, as they were officially called, defeated the South African Invitation XI twice, drew twice and lost the final game, played on 8, 9, 10 and 12 April 1976, by 122 runs, largely thanks to the bowling of Ismail 'Baboo' Ebrahim, a left-arm spinner who bowled 29.1 overs, including twelve maidens, and took 6 for 66. Moreover, the third of those wickets was his hundredth in first-class cricket and that bowling analysis was his best ever.

In *Anything But...An Autobiography*, Benaud makes particular mention of Ismail Ebrahim, whom he noted as one of the more outstanding of their opponents on the tour. He could be forgiven for not knowing that, in crossing Ebrahim's path, he was encountering a South African apartheid-imprisoned version of himself.

During the 1939–40 season, the nine-year-old Richie Benaud

went with his father, Lou, to see his first Sheffield Shield match. Father and son made the tortuous journey by various arms of public transport—a 'toast rack' tram, a bus and a train—to the Sydney Cricket Ground to see New South Wales play South Australia. After watching Clarrie Grimmett take 6 New South Wales wickets for 118 from twenty-two overs, Benaud decided, with the certainty of wide-eyed boyhood, that he would bowl leg-breaks. Although Lou Benaud forbade his son to do so for the time being because of the potential damage to young and developing muscles, the die was cast, and the young Benaud, although mostly obeying his father's dictum, knew the path ahead he wanted to follow.

In January 1957, when he was ten years old, Ismail Ebrahim had a very similar experience, although under ominously different conditions. The young Benaud had watched Clarrie Grimmett from the stairway of the Sheridan grandstand (later, the Churchill Stand). As Sidharth Monga, writing in 2011 for the ESPNcricinfo website, described it, Ebrahim's experience was somewhat different. He watched 'from the small, non-whites section at Kingsmead—[he] "couldn't go anywhere else"—[and] saw Johnny Wardle bowl Roy McLean through the gap between bat and pad'. He couldn't have put a name to it at the time, but the ball that did the damage was a 'Chinaman'.

Delivered by a left-arm bowler, the 'Chinaman' is bowled over the wrist and turns the opposite way to orthodox left-arm spin. In other words, it spins in to the right-handed batsman and away from the left-hander—from left to right on a television screen. As far as Ebrahim was concerned, that's when he said to himself, like the young Benaud had decades earlier, 'This is what I am going to do. This is what I am going to be.'

And like Richie Benaud, he worked hard at his dream. But there were obstacles in his pathway undreamed of by the young Australian when he returned home that day from the SCG full of excitement about bowling leg-breaks. As Monga records, 'According to *Wisden*, Ebrahim would have been a star in "any first-class arena". Craig Marais, former Boland [Cape Town] wicketkeeper…remembers how Ian Chappell said Ebrahim was better than any white spinner in the country.'

Benaud and Ebrahim could scarcely have had more different backgrounds and cricketing upbringings, but they shared a similar youthful fascination for the exquisitely difficult art of over-the-wrist spin and a similar determination to devote themselves to it no matter how seemingly impassable the obstacles put in their way. For Ebrahim, however, these obstacles to success were embedded in a political structure that must have seemed huge, remote and impregnable to such a young man.

'I remember the third game I played for the white club,' Ebrahim said. 'I got 10 wickets in an innings, and they insisted that I come to the pub. I said, "I don't drink, I am sorry." They asked me to just come in and have a Coke. So I thought I'd have a Coke. And there were some people [in the bar] who didn't like that idea, and so the guys told them, "If you like it, stay around. If you don't like it, you can go away. This person [Ebrahim] and we are staying here." That's how we started breaking apartheid.'

When Australia played a series in South Africa for what would be the last time before the latter's 'isolation', Ebrahim went to Sahara Stadium, Kingsmead, in Durban to watch the visitors practise. Ebrahim asked one of the Australian players if he could have a bowl and was immediately thrown a ball. Security guards intervened at once to say a black man could not bowl in the nets, but the Australians insisted, and Ebrahim rolled his arm over and promptly bowled Ian Redpath.

'Suddenly,' he recalled with a wry smile, 'it was a case of, "Who are you, my boy?" and "this and that and so forth". And to this day, Ashley Mallett, whenever he comes to South Africa, still remembers me.'

Benaud particularly mentions Ebrahim because of his outstanding performance in masterminding the International Wanderers' only defeat. But perhaps, in the athletic, handsome and youthful figure of the brilliant spinner who would never bowl his 'Chinaman' in any Test series on any famous and legendary turf, Benaud subconsciously recognised a less-privileged and star-crossed version of himself.

And he may have been moved to think in that way when he encountered some of the very difficulties that were part of Ebrahim's daily life and which Benaud had specifically sought to avoid when planning the tour. He had especially requested that there be no restrictions on where people, regardless of colour, could stand or sit to watch a game, except for members' stands, and that bars, except for those in the members' areas, be open to all. As part of his motivation was to familiarise himself with the intricacies of the South African political, social and sporting environment, he insisted on having the freedom to meet any non-white officials. He would be the sole selector of the Wanderers team, and there would be three non-white players included in the South African Invitation XI in every match. His demands, he emphasised, were not negotiable.

These conditions struck at some of apartheid's most stringent taboos: restriction of movement, no freedom of association, segregation in sporting teams, and so on. Yet so powerful was the sense of isolation, especially in sports where international competition was the height of individual and team aspirations, that Benaud's essential requirements seemed to be quickly accommodated—but not for long.

Glenn Turner, who would soon become one of New Zealand's Test batsmen, remembers buying drinks at the bar in the team hotel in Durban and being served by a woman with a Scots accent who suddenly asked him, rather loudly, about someone who had just come in. When Turner looked back to see who she meant, he saw his team mate, John Shepherd, a Barbadian, approaching the bar. The barmaid pointed theatrically and said, 'Him.'

Shepherd was embarrassed and irritated and, knowing Benaud's stated requirements for the treatment of his cricketers on and off the field, the team members present decided to ring Richie Benaud in his room to complain. Benaud immediately contacted the management and, as Turner recalls it, the bar staff and waiters all disappeared from the room, presumably, the players concluded, to attend an emergency meeting. When they returned, apologies were made and calm was restored.

Another incident, recounted by Ashley Mallett, also involved Shepherd who, it seemed, was not going to be allowed into a restaurant where the team was about to dine. In the hesitation and confusion surrounding it all, a woman walked into the restaurant with her dog without attracting any official objection. At this point, Benaud said, 'Everyone out,' and the team left.

Benaud had his own personal experience of this kind when one of the local black administrators assisting him reported that he had been refused service at a bar behind the grandstand. When he immediately followed up on this complaint, Benaud discovered that the person who had refused service was the chief of police, a large, muscular, recalcitrant man who trenchantly expressed his low opinion of Benaud and made it clear that he would do as he pleased on his own turf. When Benaud calmly assured him that this course of action would make him truly famous in a way he might not like, reconsideration was discussed and a mutually satisfactory arrangement concluded.

Mallett's and Turner's recollections could be, at a pinch, versions of the same incident. I spoke to Ashley Mallett in 2011 and to Glenn Turner in 2015, so in both cases it was a long stretch for the memory. Unquestionably, however, something like what they described did happen, and both men were adamant that Benaud acted quickly and decisively to handle a potentially very unpleasant incident and one which, above all, threatened the entire basis of the tour.

Both Turner and Mallett admired Benaud's general handling

of the team and of the tour. Turner, in particular, found him fascinating and took as many opportunities as he could to get to know him more closely. He described Benaud as unflustered, 'low-key' and 'smooth' in his dealings with the team and their hosts, and genuinely involved in a personal mission to see and understand as much as he could about apartheid South Africa. Turner had joined the tour partly to 'educate himself' about the nation and, with an Indian wife, he too had a special interest in miscegenation and the arguments surrounding and engendered by it.

Benaud, he said, made a point of trying to meet members of the Indian and black communities in every city they visited, and Turner 'tagged along' with him. Especially in Durban—the home of Ismail 'Baboo' Ebrahim, where there were big Indian and black communities—Benaud and Turner were welcomed by many of them.

Glenn Turner was a controversial figure in New Zealand cricket because he had played professionally in England and was attempting to improve on the $10.50 a day that was on offer in New Zealand. Walter Hadley, chair of New Zealand Cricket, was very critical of him, and Turner was portrayed as being in it for the money.

As Turner recalls it, 'I was supposed to be playing for the dirty dollar—not many, I might add. I had to cross over from amateurism to professionalism, and there was a strong feeling among the administration and in our country as a whole that you ought not to play for money. I had to break down a lot of barriers. And assumptions were made. One of those assumptions was about selfishness, which I totally deny.'

It was the kind of story and dispute with which Benaud was very familiar, but there was no one to collar the official and tell him what was what, and in the end conflict about payment and air fares led Turner to stay in England for his benefit season. Having met Benaud and played under his managerial control in South Africa, however, Turner decided to ask him for help.

Benaud responded generously, writing a well-informed, conciliatory and, in the end, influential letter to the New Zealand cricket administration to support Turner's case. Benaud was a powerful ally because, as Turner emphasised in discussing this phase of his career, before the 1970s most Kiwis were supporters of Australian cricket and Richie Benaud was a 'household name' in New Zealand.

Ashley Mallett also admired Benaud's stewardship of the International Wanderers, but there was, naturally enough, more history to their relationship than had been the case with Glenn Turner. As early as 1968, Mallett on his first tour was having 'finger trouble' and Benaud—who had suffered grievously from the same sort of injury until treated on tour in New Zealand— was a concerned and attentive advisor. There were other such moments in their association, as when Benaud made a special trip to help him solve problems with running on the pitch in his follow-through or when he advised a young bowler to 'get footage of Mallett and watch that', but overall Mallett found Benaud sometimes charming and sometimes aloof.

He benefited from Benaud's advice and experience, but to spurn that advice was to court some retribution. When, for example, following a discussion over dinner during which Benaud offered some firm views on how to bowl to Glenn Turner, Mallett did precisely the opposite the next day and got Turner out, according to Mallett, Benaud scarcely spoke to him for two years.

Having embarked on the tour with the deliberate and conscious aim of seeking to better understand the isolated South Africans, at least in so far as playing cricket against them might accomplish that aspiration, Benaud ended the tour with a kind of optimism. 'I have not the slightest doubt,' he said, sometime after returning, 'that in 35 days [in South Africa]...we achieved more for coloured South African cricketers than twenty years of boycotting of cricket tours could achieve.'

But, as the *Guardian* sports blogger Russell Jackson points out, Benaud was much less comforting in an address to the Cape Town Cricket Club at the end of the tour. 'I'm going back to Australia,' he concluded. 'What you do now is your own concern.' His conviction that they achieved more in their brief, eventful visit than had been accomplished by the years of boycott may have had some truth to it, but it was very much the practical man's objection to theory, the insistence that hands-on was superior to intellectualising.

It also ignored the rarely canvassed history of such cricket interventions in apartheid South Africa, of which there had been several, most notably perhaps those of the millionaire businessman, cricket patron and former Warwickshire wicket-keeper, Derrick Robins. According to ESPNcricinfo,

> The four Robins teams, in successive seasons from 1972 to 1973, were early busters of the anti-apartheid boycott and included many of the era's leading players. Robins insisted that the parties were multi-racial—John Shepherd of Kent was on the middle two trips—and shrugged off the political flak, organising trips elsewhere in the cricketing world as well.

Although many South African cricket administrators and some of the cricketers themselves regarded these trips, and especially the visit of Benaud's International Wanderers, as the beginnings of a bridge back to normal relations, the contrived nature of the tours was difficult to ignore and impossible to overlook as time passed. With visiting teams farewelled, apartheid South Africa dropped back into its usual structures and rhythms. And while John Shepherd, for example, was a very good cricketer, his frequent selection in the cause of multi-racialism made him look like a token blackfella; the uncompromising and confronting brutality of Vorster's public statements undercut the optimism of those who foresaw a coming end to isolation.

Told forcefully by Vorster that visitors to his country were expected to obey the laws of the land, Benaud had replied that he would take to heart the prime minister's exhortation especially if any of the non-negotiable conditions governing the Wanderers tour were disregarded, in which case he would return home to Australia and he would take the players with him. For his part, Ian Chappell—a canny and realistic observer, and a champion years later of recognition of the 1868 Australian Aboriginal cricket team in the Sport Australia Hall of Fame—was one of the optimists about the tour, because it seemed to him that conditions and prospects were slowly improving for indigenous South African players.

But the most clear-eyed and dampening statement came from Hassan Howa, a founding member of the South African Cricket Board of Control, which worked to promote cricket among the dispossessed and the oppressed. He lobbied for South Africa's expulsion from world sport under the slogan *No normal sport in an abnormal society*. He classed the Wanderers' tour as 'abnormal cricket', and consciously spurned the term 'multi-racial' cricket because it was 'window dressing' for visiting sporting dignitaries and campaigners. Howa's preferred terminology, 'normal cricket', meant 'cricket played by all races at all levels with equal facilities and opportunities'.

All things considered, Benaud was probably in the ranks of the optimists with his conviction that the Wanderers' thirty-five-day visit was more influential and effective for coloured South African cricketers than the long, dogged slog of protest within and beyond the tortured nation. A couple of violent and anxious decades later, with the Wanderers tour a distant, eccentric and forgotten episode, History—in the form of the newly released Nelson Mandela—crowned Protest the winner.

7

'THE MOST FAMOUS BACKYARD IN PARRAMATTA'

From Tricky Wicket to Landscaped Garden

'Like so many young Australian cricketers,
Steve Waugh began in a backyard...engaged in cutthroat
contests with his brothers...[With] the captaincy...he emerged
as an independent and radical thinker...He has been the most
successful Test captain in the history of the game.'
PETER ROEBUCK, *It Takes All Sorts*

One of the more notable golf balls in Australian sporting history
no doubt experienced the greens or sand scrapes and bunkers of
some course at some time, but it ended its days in long, repetitive
and bruising encounters with a brick tank stand and a wooden
cricket stump. Charles Williams in his *Bradman: An Australian
Hero* sets the scene:

> The boy threw a golf ball at the base of the water tank
> with his right hand while holding a cricket stump in
> his left. The ball flew back off the brickwork at an
> unpredictable angle. While it was fizzing back at him

he gripped the stump with both hands…to hit the ball before it could get past him…Even at the age of nine or ten, [he] managed to hit the golf ball with his stump, as he said himself in later life, 'more often than not'.

Wielding the stump, of course, was the young Don Bradman. He was playing his own version of that great nurturer of talent, backyard cricket. Bradman was alone as he tirelessly drove at the tank stand; but, as Steve Cannane shows in his splendid study of the subject, *First Tests: Great Australian Cricketers and the Backyards That Made Them*, all over the country and down the years, kids were playing backyard cricket—brother against brother or the boy next door, long-suffering elder brothers allowing an enthusiastic younger sister to join in, fathers flexing creaking joints to roll the arm over.

Where too-small backyards or parental strictures or the serial breaking of windows led to bans, the games would regroup in laneways or side streets: the momentum seemed unstoppable. Steve and Mark Waugh, Doug Walters and his brothers, the Chappells, Ray Lindwall and, in England, Ken Barrington, Len Hutton, Jim Laker and John Edrich all played versions of backyard cricket complete with the bespoke, often incredibly intricate rules to govern odd, challenging or downright difficult conditions. Neil Harvey played in the cobbled lanes of Fitzroy, and, long ago, as Ashley Mallett explains, before coming across from New Zealand the young Clarrie Grimmett 'played cricket with his neighbours, the Harris brothers in Roxburgh Street,

Wellington…until the gas lamps came on to brighten the gloom and Constable Thirsk arrived to clear the urchins from his presence.' Urchins they may have been, but every one of them bowled leg-breaks.

Backyard cricket, meaning an improvised, knockabout but laughingly serious version of the great game Australians flock to see in their capital cities in the bright heat of summer, continues to be widely played, especially at Christmas time and on beaches. But perhaps its glory days have passed, as space in cities becomes more cramped and side streets, lanes and byways are perceived as less safe. Steve Cannane wonders if the decline of backyard cricket might spell 'the beginning of the end of Australia's cricket dominance'. Cannane, of all people, would not be surprised to find that, unlikely as it might seem at first, a humble backyard is central to this part of our story.

No doubt it seemed like a good idea at the time. In 2008, Michael Younes was looking for a development opportunity and thought he had found one at 5 Sutherland Road, North Parramatta. For $689,000 Younes bought the property from its previous owners, David Borger and Paul Barber, and applied for a demolition order that would allow him to replace the venerable suburban bungalow with what was variously described as 'a two-storey duplex', 'a town house' or 'a dual occupancy residence'.

Younes might have recognised the potential complications in the deal, but these seemed to have been defused when the demolition order—the most vulnerable and perhaps controversial part of his program—was successful. Knocking things over, obliterating them, had become highly fraught endeavours in all of Australia's capital and regional cities. But, as Younes would discover, the devil was not so much in any particular detail of his plan as in certain events and characters which his, on the face of it, straightforward development bid resurrected from the past. For one, David Borger was no ordinary vendor.

Borger had been a councillor representing the Elizabeth Macarthur Ward from 1995 to 2008 and mayor of Parramatta— the youngest in the council's history—from 1999 to 2007. He left local government to become the Labor member for the state seat of Granville, and in that capacity he served in the Rees and Keneally administrations as Minister for Western Sydney (2008), Minister for Housing (2008–10), Minister Assisting the Minister for Transport and Roads (2009–10), and Minister for Roads (2010). Borger knew his way around housing and the local community, and had, moreover, firm views about the nature and prospects of the place he represented.

In a speech entitled 'The Power of Persuasion: How to Build a Creative City' delivered to a Currency House 'Arts and Public Life' Breakfast in Sydney in June 2007, Borger noted that governments, whether local or state, needed to think beyond economic development, to be conscious of the human as distinct from the utilitarian condition. 'As with most people who talk economic development,' he said,

> few talk about how to make Sydney's regional centres
> more interesting. Few talk about building a cultural

infrastructure and how we seed a sense of place and belonging. Attracting jobs is one thing but what about attracting people? How do we attract and retain the young, creative and talented? And so to shift these perceptions and better the quality of our civic life—and to help billboard a newly dynamic city—Parramatta has turned to its artists, [to an] ambitious arts and culture plan for the next ten years.

Not only as a vendor, then, but as a concerned, informed citizen, former mayor and sitting Member of the New South Wales Parliament, David Borger might have been expected to be aware of the cultural provenance of the property at 5 Sutherland Road, its human as distinct from utilitarian condition, its claim to being worth preserving. But even without his impressive street credentials, it would not have been difficult for Borger to recognise that in 2003, when he paid $600,100 for the house, he was dealing, as Michael Younes would be some years later, with no ordinary vendor.

The property was sold to him by the Benaud family. It had been in their possession for some sixty-five years, since the late 1930s, and had been the boyhood home of Richie and John Benaud. It was the house to which, for example, the nine-year-old Richie and his father, Lou, had returned on Saturday, 13 January 1940 after that day at the SCG where they saw Clarrie Grimmett dismiss, among others, Arthur Chipperfield and a young, up-and-coming Syd Barnes. Reportedly, both these wickets fell to Grimmett's 'flipper'. In that Sheffield Shield game between New South Wales and South Australia the spinners took 34 wickets, but one day's worth was enough for Richie Benaud. He was hooked, and he was up early the following day bowling against a brick wall.

The young Benaud bowled and bowled—prefiguring as a mere boy the awesome capacity for the sheer repetition, the attention to detail, and the physical and mental stamina that would distinguish his approach to the game as he matured. It would be some time before his muscles and tendons strengthened enough for him to undertake the difficult movements of the leg-break, but by the end of that Sunday he already had a glimpse of the spin bowler's repetitive, nagging, precise art—his total preoccupation with one small spot at the other end of the pitch where every ball bowled had to land.

As for the 'flipper': well, that was even further in the future. Despite his success with it on that day at the SCG, Clarrie Grimmett would have no opportunity to bowl the delivery in a Test match. But he taught his fellow South Australian Bruce Dooland how to bowl it, beginning one of those series of connections and encounters that were a feature of Benaud's life and career.

Described in *Wisden* as a player who 'did much to restore right-arm leg-break and googly bowling to an important place in the strategy of the game', Dooland played in only three Test matches—two against England and one against India—and when he was not selected for the 1948 Ashes tour he decided to try his luck in the Lancashire League, and from there he was invited to join county side Nottinghamshire, where he had great success as both bowler and batsman. And it was when the touring Australian team came to play Nottinghamshire in May 1956 that Dooland offered to meet Benaud before play, early on the Monday, to teach him the 'flipper'. It was a critical meeting for Benaud because Dooland, having taught and demonstrated the mechanics involved, then convinced the junior spinner to be patient, to practise the ball over and over in the nets, and to try one in a match only when he felt he had thoroughly mastered it.

Benaud had a good match against Nottinghamshire, making 62 in the first innings and taking 4 for 88—including Dooland for 1—from a solid spell of 50.3 overs, but the meeting with Dooland dwarfed even on-field success, and the lanky South Australian's graphic demonstrations, amiable style and sophisticated grasp of the art of over-the-wrist bowling made a lasting impression. As *Wisden* described him at the time, Bruce Dooland,

> like most slow bowlers, is a keen theorist delighting in experiments. In England he classes himself mainly as a wrist-spinner but, though not using his fingers so much, he finds the pitches enable him to make the ball break more sharply than in Australia. He uses the googly [more often known in Australia as the wrong 'un] sparingly, occasionally bowls a top-spinner, changes

pace and flight and deceives batsmen by employing the same action for all variations. Height and high action allow him to make the ball lift awkwardly.

As he rolled his immature arm over before the watchful eye of Lou Benaud—himself an excellent cricketer and a handy spinner, who tutored his boys in the arts of batting and bowling—in the backyard of 5 Sutherland Road on that Sunday after seeing Grimmett play, Richie Benaud was too young to be aware of the archetypal scene of which he was a part. Like most successful Australian cricketers, *Wisden* notes, 'Dooland played his early cricket as a child in the back garden. A concrete patch was the pitch and Walter Dooland, his father, encouraged him to make the ball spin.' Great players emerged from backyards and the tutelage of fathers, so such backyards might be worth preserving...

'It is the most famous backyard in Parramatta and should not be developed for units.' This was the view of Julia Finn, a Parramatta councillor and heritage-property valuer, vigorously agreeing that from Australian backyards the cricket heroes come.

The import of Michael Younes's plan to demolish the house at 5 Sutherland Road seemed to sink in slowly but, when it became clear, many voices were raised, mostly against its demolition. As the controversy gathered momentum, an application to the state government to place an interim heritage order on the property was rejected, to the profound disappointment of Lord Mayor

Paul Garrard, who was 'shocked and disappointed' at Planning Minister Tony Kelly's decision that the house's 'level of association' with Richie Benaud did not justify a heritage classification. David Borger's bona fides were questioned. How could he not have known that Younes was a developer?

Garrard was scathing, and it became clear that old enmities and political baggage were now part of what to many seemed a simple and straightforward move to preserve an important and evocative site: 'Demolition Dave [Borger] did what he wanted to do and sold out to developers…He's got quite a hide. He knew what this developer was going to do.' To which Borger replied: 'If Garrard thinks it important to heritage list the house, it has been open to him for a long time to do so. What makes this issue important to him is not the house, but the fact I part-owned it. What's happening here is that Garrard, as we have come to expect, is playing the person and not the issue.'

'This shocking decision has let everyone down,' Garrard said. 'Richie Benaud is a Parramatta icon and known around the world for his achievements both on and off the pitch. Behind Don Bradman, he is Australia's most famous cricketer and it would be a sad day if his family home, the place where his skills were first honed, was to be ever re-developed.' But the cat was out of the bag, and only the affection and loyalty of some ordinary people rang really true as argument and counter-argument raged through the pages of the *Parramatta Advertiser*.

'I worked for the Benauds occasionally as a gardener and lawn mower when Mr Benaud wasn't well,' wrote Wayne

Cowan. 'It was an honour and Mr and Mrs Benaud were very kind. I enjoyed discussing cricket with Mr Benaud. The house and garden were beautifully maintained by them. It was thrilling to stand in the backyard where history was made. Please don't destroy this Parramatta and Australian icon.'

And from Rachel came a balanced and considered plea that found many supporters:

> This house should be saved. It is a disgrace that we are not preserving properties with important history for future generations. As far as Australia is concerned, we have a terrible track record for bulldozing our architectural heritage...Parramatta council is allowing way too many of the older homes to be knocked down; very soon they are going to have a big ugly grey city on their hands.

Meanwhile, a suggestion from councillor Tony Issa that the council buy the property in partnership with Cricket Australia and the New South Wales state government found no support but also led to Issa's realising that more complex and conflicting forces lay beneath the surface of what had looked like an effort to honour the Benauds and especially Richie. As reported in the *Parramatta Advertiser*, Issa speculated:

> Councillor Garrard is using the issue as a political football to disparage his old sparring partner, Granville

MP, David Borger, who sold the house to Michael Younes…Whether ratepayers would appreciate their money being used to acquire the property is hard to determine. After all, not all people are cricket fanatics. However our councillors clearly passed up the most direct route of saving the house. Even brothers Richie and John Benaud, while expressing disappointment [about the possible demolition] have not bought the property back. Mr Younes, then, must be respected for his offer to build a memorial to the site. He has acted within the law from the outset, and didn't need to offer this olive branch. For Parramatta councillors and other opponents, it's time they put their money where their mouth is.

As a peace offering in a rapidly deteriorating situation, Michael Younes had proposed to erect on the property

a sandstone wall built from the foundations of the current house, commemorating the great contribution the Benauds have made to this community. Council may wish to submit a memorial plaque to be placed on this wall. This construction will be paid for by me in good faith and at no cost to council. In return I expect my development application to be assessed on its merits and not on political motives.

Younes's parting shot clearly demonstrates that he too was convinced he had fallen into a battle between political adversaries whose disputes seemed to outweigh and diminish the actual argument about heritage and community legacy. Issa had accused colleague councillors of 'grandstanding' and seeking 'media attention' but being unwilling to act when the time came for decisions. Younes was banking on his reasonably generous gesture being a deal breaker. But he was wasting his time.

The proposal was rejected by Garrard, who said, 'We can't have developers coming in and saying, "We'll do this if you let us knock it over." When we make a decision…then we'll consider the terms.'

In the end, after the controversy had become tedious and stalemated, there were no winners, not even Michael Younes, whose original ideas were scarcely realised. The Benaud home at 5 Sutherland Road made way for an 'Executive Brand New Home with Contemporary Architecture'. It promised to 'fulfil the dreams of purchasers who are looking for high-quality stylish life, situated at a most sought after street in this "Dress Circle" area'. The new owners would enjoy an 'Exceptional sun-drenched large lounge room and dining room with high-quality timber floor throughout, access to open plan large alfresco, great for entertaining', as well as a 'Gourmet Polyurethane Kitchen with stainless steel appliances, 40mm Caesar stone bench, 5 burner gas cook tops, ducted range hood, custom pantry, built in dishwasher & all joinery fitted with soft closing drawers and cupboard doors', and '4 large size bedrooms all with built-in wardrobes, huge master bedroom with en suite and walk in wardrobe, access to the balcony', and many other amenities and marvels of modern living.

The 'Fantastic private entertaining landscaped garden, with easy maintenance', however, was too genteel for quick singles and would not be at all suitable as a shortened cricket pitch, though the story goes that on the night of Richie's death, ghostly joyous cries of 'Owzat!', 'Catch!' and 'Well bowled!' drifted across the neat suburban lawn and out into the vast arena of the skies.

8

THE FRENCH CONNECTION

Sportsmanship, Style and Tenacity

'The Huguenot characteristics were to be prideful, diligent and...honest. They were cheerful, artistic, individualistic...and courteous, hospitable, humorous...and they had the ingenuity to make a plan.' CELIA-JOY MARTINS, *Fire & Ashes—Iron & Clay*

'There is a delightful, quiet village called Benaud in France near Clermont-Ferrand on the D229...It is a hamlet which doesn't appear in the French telephone system...despite the village name there are no Benauds living in that area.' RICHIE BENAUD, 'The Benaud Connection'

'Owzat?' Richie Benaud's appeal was vociferous, loud and seemingly irresistible. Not surprising, since his personal example was introducing into Australian cricket a pleasing lack of inhibition, a freedom to celebrate and gesture and express emotion—especially joy and achievement and excitement—that was new to the Australian game at first-class level, even if it was bread and butter on innumerable local ovals in the heat of a late Saturday afternoon.

This particular appeal, however, was different. It was not instant but followed a sort of split-second puzzled pause, and it was not echoed all around the field by his team, many of whom also seemed nonplussed. The unusual hesitation was because the West Indian opening batsman Joe Solomon had successfully and firmly defended the top-spinner that Richie Benaud had tossed up to him. It was the next few seconds that would turn forward defence into a temporary sensation, with the Australian captain firmly at its centre.

Benaud's strident appeal may have been an example of Huguenot cussedness. Richie Benaud regarded himself as a Huguenot descendant—even though the 'B' list of Huguenot-connected Australian surnames on the official Huguenot website has no 'Benaud' where there should be one: 'Baud, Bédard, Beehag (Behague), Bellett, Bernard...' Certainly his forebears, as he describes them, are not only unarguably French but also seem to have had that quality of determination and life-against-the-odds that distinguished the Huguenots centuries earlier in their sturdy Protestantism, their resistance to Catholic oppression and, eventually, their choice of escape in large numbers from France to the Netherlands, England, Ireland, Germany and Switzerland.

According to the Huguenot Society of Australia, they 'went to any country that would take them, allow them religious freedom and the chance to work to support themselves and their families'. They were seeking refuge, and the word 'refugee'—so familiar to us in the twenty-first century—entered the language to describe their plight.

'Everywhere they went they brought with them their religion, their considerable artistic and industrial skills, and their habits of hard work and civic responsibility. They made good citizens—as so many refugees do if given the chance—and their loss was a great blow to France.'

That was in earlier times, but Louis Ferdinand Branxton Benaud and Richard Grainger Napoleon Benaud, who left their native France and sailed to Australia, perhaps not escaping persecution so much as seeking fresh pastures and better opportunities, were Huguenot-like in their intrepidity, and they were tough, innovative workers—Louis founded a newspaper, the *Richmond River Herald*, and Richard, a successful jeweller and watchmaker, founded a dynasty. He was Richie Benaud's grandfather.

Who can say what precisely were the talents bequeathed to Richie and his brother, John, through the pioneering determination of the Savilles on their mother's side, and the Gallic panache of the Benauds? It was a rich mix and riches duly followed. One of these endowments, quite apart from obvious sporting ability, was an innate sense of sportsmanship and fair play.

John Benaud was an accomplished cricketer who played three Tests for Australia, topscoring with 142 in the second innings of one of them. As captain of the New South Wales team, he was astute, capable, led from the front and was his own man. When Cricket NSW demanded he stop wearing Adidas Grass Sports shoes, he refused to obey and was suspended for a month, despite his outstanding captaincy and performances. His stand was so palpably reasonable and resolute that the incident became a cause célèbre, and the administrators were forced to back down. This was a typical reaction from a Benaud, combining sturdy common sense with an insistence on individuality and self-esteem. No doubt John Benaud didn't need a model, but he had one anyway in big brother Richie.

Richie Benaud's sportsmanship was evident and admired from early in his career. His demeanour on the field, his attractive, sometimes swashbuckling batting, and his obvious enjoyment not only of his own feats but also of those of his team mates were all suggestive of a free spirit, a player absorbed in, and by, the wonders of a contest he loved and respected. As the Australian captain he clearly approved of, and to a large extent helped introduce to the game, on-field congratulations between players and a general, acceptable level of extroversion, although the much older Benaud not long ago noted the deterioration of genuine on-field ebullience into subtle denigration when he remarked during a West Indies–Australia Test that 'ironic clapping and the blowing of kisses [to departing batsmen] seem to be characteristics of recent cricket'.

Just as John Benaud's unpretentious individuality brought him into head-on conflict with cricket officialdom, so his elder brother's meticulous, caring attitude towards this 'finest' of games, one which was for him character-building and a potential source of harmony between nations, occasionally manifested itself as rather stern and unbending.

Which brings us back to Joe Solomon's forward defence during the Second Test of the West Indies' extraordinary 1960–61 tour of Australia. As Solomon played Benaud's top-spinner his cap fell onto the stumps, dislodging a bail. When he saw this, Benaud appealed. The batsman was technically out and the umpire, as he had to, gave Solomon out 'hit wicket'. The West Indian all-rounder Garfield Sobers said the decision was correct, but the huge crowd thought differently, and the Australians, in particular their captain, were roundly booed and howled at with an energy, reverberation and prolonged enthusiasm that seem especially the preserve of the great and packed expanses of the MCG terraces and grandstands.

Ruefully recalling the incident, Benaud reckoned that only eleven of the seventy thousand people present did not boo him. Arguments and intense discussions about sportsmanship and the spirit of the game ensued for days and, as always on such occasions, the ghost of Vinoo Mankad hovered around the debates and controversies. Benaud's action was compared— unfairly it must be said—to Mankad's famous dismissal of Bill Brown at the SCG in the Second Test of India's 1947 tour of Australia. With Brown backing up at the non-striker's end and already well down the pitch, Mankad suddenly cut short his approach to the crease and ran the batsman out. But this was actually a reprise.

As reported by 'Ginty' Lush in the *Age*, 'the first time [Mankad] had Brown at his mercy—in an India versus Australian XI match at the SCG—he beckoned the batsman back with a crooked finger when Brown was already well out of his ground. This was hailed as one of the most sporting acts ever seen at the SCG.' When, a few overs later, Brown again advanced several long paces down the pitch, Mankad stopped in his delivery stride and ran him out.

In the Test match, the Mankad run-out of Bill Brown was done without warning. 'Doing a Mankad' entered the language of cricket to describe an act generally regarded as technically legitimate but against the spirit of the game and would still be seen as such even in these tough days when sledging, intimidation and various forms of confrontation on the pitch are common and to a large extent accepted as inevitable. Steve Waugh, as captain of the Australian Test team, made an effort to normalise intimidatory behaviour by describing it as 'mental disintegration', but the means and the look of it were not essentially changed. It was still confrontation of one kind or another.

Richie Benaud's appeal when Solomon's cap fell on to the stumps was clearly a long way short of intimidation. It was a highly excited, spur-of-the-moment reaction which, on reflection, he might not have repeated if he had his time over again but, on the other hand, he might have because Benaud was admirably consistent in his handling of the game's sportsmanship and spirit moments. Facing the television camera two decades later after the infamous 'underarm' incident, he conceded that there would be many opinions and much disagreement about what had just happened, but his own view—straightforward and crisply stated before his curt 'Good night' issued on behalf of Channel Nine's Wide World of Sports—was that it was 'a disgraceful performance' and 'one of the worst things I have ever seen done on a cricket field'.

Benaud's approach to another highly volatile and contentious problem—throwing—was similarly uncomplicated. As the controversy gathered heat and a great deal of fuzziness in the early 1960s, with much of both the enlightenment and the obfuscation revolving around the figure of the Australian fast bowler Ian Meckiff, Benaud attended a dinner hosted by Sir Donald Bradman for the available Sheffield Shield captains: Ken Mackay, Barry Shepherd and Bill Lawry. (South Australia's Les Favell was playing in Brisbane but Benaud discussed the meeting with him later.) The topic of the after-dinner discussion was 'suspect actions', illustrated by films Bradman had collected.

It seems to have been a watershed moment for Benaud because, as a result of the discussions and Bradman's demonstrations, he reached two uncompromising conclusions: one was that if one of his bowlers was called for throwing by an umpire, he would not continue to be part of the attack; and the second, broader still, was that, as captain, Benaud would not bowl anyone even suspected of having a dubious action.

This firm resolve came to its inevitable crisis point in the opening Test of the series against South Africa in 1963–64. On 7 December, when South Africa began its first innings chasing Australia's 435, Ian Meckiff was no-balled four times in his first over by umpire Colin Egar. Benaud removed Meckiff from the attack and did not bowl him again. The shattered fast bowler, with figures for the game of one over, no maidens, no wicket for 8, retired from all cricket when that First Test ended in a rain-interrupted draw on Wednesday, 11 December.

The result was immediate and tumultuous. Meckiff's selection in the team for the First Test, Egar's calls, Benaud's reaction, furious point–counterpoint arguments in the Australian press, and a flurry of protests from the cricket-following public— 'Why didn't he bowl Meckiff from the other end to see if Lou Rowan would no-ball him?' 'Why did they pick Meckiff at all?' 'Meckiff was set up so they could show they're against chuckers'—were all ingredients in a massive and volatile mixture of conspiracy theory and fact, fiction and the impregnable confidence of pub talk.

Through it all, Benaud remained calm, argued only when he had to and stuck to his convictions, but he was under no illusion about how portentous the events had been. It was, all things considered, a disaster whatever way it was regarded, and a pall seemed to descend sadly on both teams and the crowd in the immediate aftermath of that dismal over. In the contentious days that followed, Benaud knew how profoundly Meckiff was hurt; he knew that Meckiff's family were deeply disturbed, and that a close friendship between Meckiff and Egar had possibly been endangered.

Nevertheless, there was steel and occasional asperity in Benaud's intellectual and philosophical position on the question of throwing. When he had captained New South Wales in a Shield match against South Australia in January 1963, he was taken to task by the chairman of selectors, Dudley Seddon, for not giving Gordon Rorke more overs. Rorke was part of the New South Wales pace attack, along with Frank Misson and

Alan Davidson. It was Benaud's opinion that Rorke's action was suspect and possibly from time to time illegitimate. In the match Rorke bowled only three overs in the first innings and four in the second. But fellow pacemen Davidson and Misson between them bowled only twenty-four in the whole match. Spinners Benaud and Martin did the work and the damage—Benaud, 4 for 46 off eleven overs in the first innings and 6 for 52 off twenty-six in the second; Martin, 4 for 43 off twelve and 2 for 61 off sixteen.

So powerful and pervasive was the preoccupation with and the fear of chucking at the time, however, that the merest whiff of it was enough to cause disproportionate disturbance. Seddon told Benaud to remember in future that his position was captain: the selectors would deal with bowlers' legitimacy or otherwise. It was obviously a tense conversation, almost a stand-off.

Benaud was being true to his vow made as a result of that evening's discussion with Bradman and the fellow state captains. Unimpressed by Seddon's appeal to authority, Benaud pulled some rank in return, telling him that he would categorically refuse to bowl any bowler with the merest tendency to a suspect action. His parting shot was that if the point needed to be made more trenchantly, he would promote such a bowler and open the batting with him! The selectors could respond any way they wished.

John Benaud's stand against New South Wales cricket officialdom a decade or so later was characterised, like his brother's, by the same quality of unflinching determination to stick to principles which he had personally arrived at and saw to be reasonable, and by a challenging refusal to be browbeaten or pushed around by bureaucrats or cricket ideologues.

These are not exclusively Huguenot characteristics, but they are powerfully reminiscent of those redoubtable, venturesome Benaud ancestors, Louis Ferdinand Branxton Benaud and Richard Grainger Napoleon Benaud. As well as their personal talents and gifts, they brought with them to the other side of the world their religion. For Lou Benaud and his two sons, the religion was cricket.

PART
III

9

'MARVELLOUS!'

The Voice of Cricket

'Put your brain into gear and if you can add to what's
on the screen then do it, otherwise shut up.'
RICHIE BENAUD on commentating

Richie Benaud's calculated and perfectly gauged reticence was
a feature from the very start of Channel Nine's cricket coverage, as it had been during his commentary career in England,
but what appears to his vast audience of Australian fans to be
a natural affinity for the microphone and the television camera
was the result of some sacrifice and a lot of hard work, training
and dedication.

At the end of the 1956 Ashes tour, the Australians played two
matches against Scotland, one at Mannofield Park in Aberdeen
and the other at Hamilton Crescent Ground in Glasgow. In
Aberdeen, Benaud took 2 for 24 in the first innings and 6 for

34 in the second. In Glasgow, he opened the batting with Neil Harvey and made 47, and took 2 for 32. All in all, it was a pleasant, not-too-serious conclusion to what had been something of a nightmare tour for the Australians. They drew the First and Fifth Tests, and won the Second by 185 runs. In the Third, however, they were beaten by an innings and 42 runs; and, in the Fourth, the infamous Old Trafford dustbowl on which Laker took 19 wickets, they lost by an innings and 185 runs.

Benaud had a modest tour with the ball and, apart from a splendid 97 in the Second Test, managed to pass 30 only twice. Not surprisingly, the whole playing group was eagerly looking forward to the three-week break that was to follow the Scotland games. Benaud may also have been looking forward to it, but he had very different plans from the travelling and relaxing of his team mates. As he details in *My Spin on Cricket*, he rented a monastically small room at the Royal Automobile Club, paid all his own expenses and embarked on a television training course organised for him by Tom Sloan, whom Benaud refers to as 'BBC's Head of Light Entertainment'.

Sloan would actually not be head until 1961; nevertheless, Benaud could not have chosen a better mentor. He was an experienced and innovative television and radio broadcaster with a string of international and local BBC programs already to his credit. He had the vision and the reach in the industry to ensure that the young Benaud saw every aspect of the business of covering news, sport and entertainment for television. But perhaps even more importantly for the aspiring student under his tutelage, Sloan was intent on toughening the tone and character of British light entertainment.

Just as on the stage playwrights in the 1950s and early 1960s were rebelling against the polite 'drawing room' drama of Noel Coward and Terence Rattigan with plays like *Look Back in Anger*, *Roots* and *A Taste of Honey*, on television Sloan was looking for realism in comedy, a more stringent connection to ordinary—and especially working-class—life. Under his direction, Tony Hancock (*Hancock's Half Hour*), Harry H. Corbett and Wilfred Bramble (*Steptoe and Son*), and the writers of both shows, Ray Galton and Alan Simpson, would transform English comedy on the small screen.

When Richie Benaud embarked on the course Sloan had mapped out for him, these innovations were still in the future, but the attitude, vision and determined ideological fervour that would encourage them were Sloan's way. Whatever else he took from his mentor, Benaud could not but be deeply influenced by Sloan's dedication to his craft, his capacity for work, his attention to detail and, perhaps above all, his openness to change and to risk-taking. These characteristics helped to revolutionise BBC TV Light Entertainment in the 1960s and, through Richie Benaud, Sloan's willing, observant and sharp-thinking pupil, they would eventually play a role in the thorough overhauling of television cricket commentary in Australia.

Benaud's broadcasting and television pedigree was also shaped and influenced by other important and adept masters of the art. One of these was 'the voice of Wimbledon', Dan Maskell, saluted in his obituary as 'one of the BBC's most respected commentators on any sport' with a style of tennis commentary that was 'gentle, unhurried, non-panicky'.

Like many sports commentators Maskell had stock remarks that became his signature and that passed for a time into the vernacular of the day. At his peak and especially during the two weeks of the Wimbledon championship, his favourite phrases—a 'dream of a backhand', 'quite extraordinary' and, expressive of genteelly restrained incredulity, 'Oh, I say'—became the stuff of everyday chat, pub talk and satire.

Another man behind the microphone whom Benaud admired, studied and learned from was Henry Longhurst, the gun golf commentator on BBC television from the late 1950s until his death in 1978. Commentating on the leading tournaments in Britain and the United States, Longhurst was known for his graphic wit—'He's all hands and wrists, like a man dusting furniture'—and his erudite commitment to the beauties and terrors of golf. His call of Jack Nicklaus's freakish birdie putt at the 16th in the 1975 US Masters Tournament—'My, my… in all my life I have never seen a putt quite like that'—became a kind of perennial catchphrase for that hole, though no doubt Longhurst would have eclipsed his own fame had he lived to see and attempt to describe Tiger Woods' phenomenal pitch at the same hole in 2005.

Quite apart from his role for Benaud as a matchless exemplar at the microphone and in front of the camera, Longhurst had a huge range of friends and contacts. Among those in his circle and closest to him was the cricket writer and commentator Jim Swanton.

There are, of course, any number of ways that the young Richie Benaud would have crossed paths with Swanton, both in those vital three weeks when he was doing his course with Tom Sloan and in the years following during his return visits to England as an Australian Test cricketer. However it came about, his meeting Swanton was vital beyond any consideration of professional development as writer and broadcaster.

Swanton's secretary was, in Ian Wooldridge's words, 'the demure and elegant Daphne Surfleet'. According to Wooldridge she was the

> first woman to enter an English cricket Press box...
> introduced at Lord's by the great E. W. Swanton
> glowering defiance at anyone who dared object to this
> monumental breach of protocol. She is now Mrs Richie
> Benaud—they married in 1967—and for the last 30 years
> has been known to everyone in the game as Daffers.

And then there was Peter O'Sullevan—another famous voice—this time the voice of racing. Sue Mott, in her *Daily Telegraph* encomium for O'Sullevan's ninetieth birthday, conjured the timbre, richness and seductiveness of that voice, its

> magnificent authority, mellifluous beauty, grammati-
> cal proficiency and a hint of drollery...It is not just the

'Voice of Racing'…it is the voice of voices. For more than 50 years, on a variety of airwaves, this glorious instrument…instructed us upon our victories and our losses (the latter, by far, predominating) with the accuracy of an obsessive and the compassion of a fellow-sufferer. The sound of Sir Peter calling the horses should be one of our exports into outer space to signify the depth of our civilisation.

O'Sullevan's call of Red Rum's third Grand National win in 1977 is remembered for producing just about the best-known piece of televised sports commentary ever. As Red Rum stormed to the line, O'Sullevan captured the moment: 'It's hats off and a tremendous reception, you've never heard one like it at Liverpool…and Red Rum wins the National!'

As the story goes, Peter O'Sullevan greeted the young Richie Benaud with his characteristic amiability, but with one rule that would govern their two days together. 'Don't speak to me. At all. During the day.' Benaud of course agreed and embarked on two days' silence, which was only broken when they knocked off on day two and discussed their work over a few beers. Benaud never forgot the meticulous organisation and preparation that O'Sullevan routinely put into his broadcasting and television presentations. Just as Tom Sloan had intended, it was another masterclass.

For a twenty-six-year-old abroad for the first time and on the brink of what looked like being, with a bit of luck, an outstanding career as a cricketer, Benaud's decision to devote his three-week break to taking Tom Sloan's training course was remarkably disciplined, an aspect of his innate aspiration to establish as much control as possible over events and circumstances. And it was critical. Without that course and those crowded three weeks, as he later conceded, his whole life would have been very different. As it was, it would be seven years before his efforts and sacrifice—he could after all have joined the team on a European holiday—bore fruit in the commentary opportunities that would make him as illustrious in the field as any of his mentors.

It was not only the course itself: it was also the new world which Tom Sloan's imaginative and fearlessly experimental approach to sports programming had opened up for him that shocked, excited and energised the young Benaud in ways that were confronting, even for someone as prescient and calculating about future possibilities as he was. But once invited into the realm, Benaud met and voraciously learned from commentating royalty.

His close attention to the words, ways and writings of Longhurst and Maskell during the English summers of 1953, 1956, 1960 and 1961 and his two long, silent days with O'Sullevan at Newbury in 1956 were undergraduate and postgraduate courses crammed together. The hours were long, the pressure intense and the lessons, for future reference, were abundant, but if there was one characteristic that these eloquent talkers shared it was reticence. They never said too much, mostly they said just enough or perhaps just short of enough, leaving irony, pregnant pause or rhythm to do the rest.

The close, frequent and intense exposure to the work of such masters of their trade must also have made certain subconscious if indefinable impressions: the value and importance of controlled repetition, for example; the role and importance of cadence, the effect of emphases carefully deployed, and the way sheer quality and variety of voice and tone could bring alive a description or make a comment memorable or surprising or give it irresistible charm. And there were the unteachable extras that so distinguished the great commentators—a recognisable, endearing and inimitable personality, the development of a distinctive personal style, and an aptitude with language and the vernacular, especially as applied to a particular sport. Maskell's 'dream of a backhand', Longhurst's 'In all of my life I've never seen a putt like that' and O'Sullevan's famous salute to Red Rum were for Benaud only moments in a whole pattern of memories, tips, suggestions and invaluable work experience in the presence of the most seasoned of performers in the field.

Maskell, Longhurst and O'Sullevan were also journalists, writers of some note. Alastair Cooke said of Longhurst that he had 'a prose style...as effortless as falling out of bed'; and of O'Sullevan, Sue Mott remarked he was 'a purveyor of felicitous sentences, both in speech and print'. Longhurst's autobiography, *My Life and Soft Times*, in which, among other things, he took to task George Orwell for his attack in 'Such, Such Were the Joys' on St Cyprian's, the school they both attended, was a critical and popular success, the product of a 'forensic memory'.

Benaud was well aware of his mentors' literary claims and

fame. He was a print journalist himself and, not long before his three weeks with the BBC, had worked on the *Sun* doing police rounds under the supervision of Noel Bailey. Described by the veteran *Sun* and *Daily Mirror* reporter Frank Crook as one of the *Sun*'s 'tough nuts', Bailey, 'beefy and bellicose, led the paper's crime coverage'. It would not be long before Benaud chanced his own literary arm, publishing books in the first three years of the 1960s: *Way of Cricket* (1961), the splendid *A Tale of Two Tests* (1962) and *Spin Me a Spinner* (1963).

It's not too difficult to see the influence of this diversity of mentors and experiences in the finished work of art that was Richie Benaud, the voice of televised cricket. We can detect the influence of Maskell's calm, gentle, measured delivery in Benaud's smooth, eminently listenable Australian rhythms and, although no doubt he did not consciously seek a catchphrase of his own, his 'Marvellous!' and 'What a catch!' and 'Tew for tew tew tew' have entered the language as surely as any of his avatars' trademark exclamations.

As a writer he was spare and pointed, profoundly influenced by the economy of words that he had noticed in and learned from Maskell, Longhurst and O'Sullevan. As a professional presenter of television, he displayed the perfectionism, intensity of preparation and cultivation of a personal style that he had seen in professionals like Swanton, Brian 'Jonners' Johnston, Peter West and, possibly above all, Tom Sloan.

On screen, Benaud was cool, basically unemotional but no zombie, and unremitting in his regard for, and demonstration of, high standards and peerless quality. And it was Sloan, quietly, relentlessly fighting his own battles within the BBC for artistic, especially comedic, revolution, who perhaps above all showed Benaud how to look for, find and then tread the television paths of change, individuality and excellence.

10

SPEAKING MY MIND

Richie Benaud in Prose

'History does not record itself. It requires will and effort
and craft and care to keep the past from fading.'
GIDEON HAIGH, *The Summer Game*

Richie Benaud trained as a journalist, but someone with his lively mind and innovative views would not be confined to short articles and straight reporting, and it was not long before he turned his attention to some more extended writing. In the unpretentious *Way of Cricket* (1961), he begins plotting a literary course and developing a narrative mode that would become consistently and attractively his own. *Way of Cricket* begins with a determined, even slightly Preface:

> There are no dressing room scandals 'lifting the lid off' cricket, nor violent blasting criticisms, in this book...I

feel that the average cricket follower has far more perception and sense of fair play than he is often given credit for…[Over] the years there have been both good and bad things taking place in the centre and even in the outer—but even in its leanest times the good things of cricket will far outweigh the bad.

Here Benaud's explicit distancing of himself and his writing from any suggestion of scandal-mongering or personality-cultism—in sharp contrast to growing trends in sports reporting at the time—signals a stance he will maintain and, if anything, intensify in subsequent books. As the Preface to *Way of Cricket* unfolds, the forthrightness and pragmatic tone of its opening paragraphs are quietly re-enforced.

He lays before the reader an unadorned plan of action promising a relaxed, conversational mode leavened with some unobtrusive instruction. His qualifications for presuming to consider and discuss the way of cricket appear in a slightly self-deprecatory curriculum vitae—he has been a captain, a player, and a veteran of most of cricket's high and low moments, and has been dealt the deceptive hand of personal successes and failures that is the lot of those who play the game.

Prefiguring a position to which he will remain committed with strange determination for the rest of his life, and consistent with *Way of Cricket*'s strident rejection of insider populism, he emphasises for the first time and certainly not for the last that he is not writing autobiography. A few books and many years later, he will repeat this assurance with even greater emphasis in the title of his 1998 book, *Anything But...An Autobiography*.

The tentativeness of the inexperienced author is evident in Benaud's concern to make clear what the book is not. So gossip, autobiography, coaching manual, dressing-room sensationalism are all firmly seen off in favour of a practical, comprehensive look at the game of cricket threaded with some deliberately meandering reminiscence on memorable players and matches. It is a format that he will perfect and that will serve him well as he develops into a cricket writer and thinker of note, and it conforms with—and may have been distantly and lightly influenced by—the great C. L. R. James's views on cricket writing:

> Writing critically about West Indian cricket and cricketers, or any cricket for that matter, is a difficult discipline. The investigation, the analysis, even the casual historical or sociological gossip about any great cricketer should deal with actual cricket, the way he bats or bowls or fields, does all or any of these. You may wander far from where you started, but unless you have your eyes constantly on the ball, in fact never take your eyes off it, you are soon not writing about cricket, but yourself (or other people) and psychological or literary responses to the game. This can be and has been done quite brilliantly, adding a little something to literature but practically nothing to cricket, as little as

the story of Jack and the Beanstalk (a great tale) adds
to our knowledge of agriculture.

Benaud's second book, *A Tale of Two Tests*, appeared in the
following year, 1962. Perhaps because it was powered by his
imaginative treatment of memorable personal experience, it
represented a startling advance on *Way of Cricket* in which the
matter-of-fact approach and almost over-sensitive avoidance
of the temptations of insider revelations—true to the Jamesian
'eyes-on-the-ball' principle—were constraining.

In *A Tale of Two Tests*, these documentary restraints are
replaced by real narrative skill, descriptive flair and sensitive awareness of atmosphere. His evocation of some typical
Manchester weather, its peculiarly intense wintriness and its
funereal lack of colour despite the actual season, establishes the
tone and mood as he prepares to tell the story of that Fourth
Test at Old Trafford in 1961. Similarly, his tale of the Tied Test
captures all the drama, surprises, unbelievable skills, camaraderie and intensity of those amazing five days of cricket.

When *Spin Me a Spinner* appeared in 1963, Benaud had
published three books in three years and, although his exploits,
success and daring as a captain and player were what had characterised him above all, he was beginning to establish himself as
an articulate and shrewd commentator on the game. After his
retirement as a player in 1964, however, he was increasingly
preoccupied with newspaper work, television in England and,
in due course, his commitments with Channel Nine in Australia.

So, although he wrote regularly for the *News of the World* and his name appears in many publications over those years as a generous writer of forewords to other peoples' cricket books, six years passed after *Spin Me a Spinner* before the appearance of *Willow Patterns* in 1969, and there was another, far longer gap—aside from books that gave accounts of specific seasons—that was packed with incident and vaulting change and controversy in the world of televised cricket before the publication of *The Appeal of Cricket* in 1995, in which he canvasses the tenor of the rapidly changing landscape of cricket since the mid-1980s, characteristically interleaving the account with some remembered matches and personalities.

The introduction to *Anything But...An Autobiography*, published in 1998, suggests that this book, although broadly following the pattern of its predecessors, occupies a subtly different place in Benaud's now considerable oeuvre. In discussing the title—to which his friend Bob Gray contributed more or less inadvertently in conversation—Benaud muses on what could accurately be called his fortunate life or, conversely his unfortunate life during which illness and especially injury had played their part. Any of these lines of thought could have contributed to the title.

Or again, he could have taken his cue from the close interweaving in his life story of cricket and the media, with some emphasis on how, through extraordinary interventions of good and bad luck, with Benaud admitting he was the recipient of most of the good luck, he had become Australia's Test captain. It is not appropriate self-deprecation alone that prompts Benaud's admission that his is a story stretching credulity—so much falls so neatly into place. Norm O'Neill caught just the right note as the players celebrated the Old Trafford victory. He invited Benaud to hop into the bath fully clothed. With his luck, O'Neill assured his captain, he wouldn't even get wet. But no one who closely followed Benaud's career needs to be reminded that sheer talent, inspiration, dogged intent, flashes of genius and profound self-confidence outweighed luck in his successful story, however far-fetched the script might have seemed at times.

On the book's front cover, Benaud, a betting man, or perhaps his publishers, had two bob each way. The words 'Richie Benaud' and 'An Autobiography' appear in large gold letters. But poised between the author's name and the title, in white lowercase and in smaller type, is 'Anything But'. As with his opinion of biography—'one is enough'—Benaud's firm view about autobiography lay behind these equivocations. He saw an autobiography as marking the end of a career and, at that stage of his life, he was not at all ready to send such a signal.

It is not clear exactly what Bob Gray's aversion was to autobiography, or why Richie Benaud found it persuasive enough to follow to the letter, but there's no question that *Anything But...An Autobiography* is indeed anything but an autobiography. Answering Gray's question about his activities, Benaud confirms that there is another book on the way, and he clearly and unambiguously includes Daphne in the project. So she too, presumably, agreed with Gray's constraint.

Certainly the first couple of chapters—'The Benauds and the Savilles: Pioneers' and 'Lou Benaud: Cricket and Other Things'—vividly recreate the family's past. And chapters three and four—'Big School for a Little Boy' and 'Up a Level But Can I Handle It?'—trace Richie's boyhood and his beginnings in schoolboy cricket. The emphases and the rhythms of the account gradually and ineluctably shift, however, to his life in cricket and, as the title promises, away from personal recollection and revelation, although incidents from the past, pre-eminently an impressively candid and unadorned reference to the breakdown of his first marriage, occasionally surface as what is essentially and ultimately a cricket book—and, characteristically, a good and lively one—unfolds.

Anything But...An Autobiography marks an important stage in Benaud's literary output because it deals with a question that had clearly been on his mind since he first began to write. How much should his personal life and achievements—in short, autobiographical considerations and episodes—thread through his work? The unequivocal position adopted and explicitly set out in *Way of Cricket* gradually softens, but the question of self-esteem, his changing status in the story he pieces together as the books emerge, nags at him until he firmly confronts it in *Anything But...An Autobiography.*

Even there, however, the very title, suggested to him by someone who apparently really did mean what he said—'Not an autobiography. Anything but an autobiography, Benaud'— is evading the question: Do I write about myself, openly and unwaveringly, or don't I? The answer is a compromise. The early chapters deal with his forebears and their interesting French and Australian origins, his own early days as a junior but very promising cricketer, and the precariousness of employment for young men constantly going absent to play cricket. At about that point, the compromise cuts in and the structure becomes more reminiscent of that early form which allowed Benaud to digress and indulge in reminiscences of great players and memorable matches.

Nevertheless, *Anything But...An Autobiography* is a finely written but often tough and personal cricket memoir which returns with affecting and gentle tact to the autobiographical theme at its conclusion. Along the way, when necessary, it is a book in praise of talent, fairness and friendship, and in merciless denunciation of hypocrisy, disloyalty and pretension. Espoused explicitly and almost aggressively in his first book, this is the characteristic Benaud literary method—an almost severe commitment to prose that scorns adornment but can accommodate a nice turn of irony, a quiet, sometimes acerbic wit, and can 'wander off' now and then into 'strictly cricketing' reminiscence or character portrayal.

But it is also a style in which the single-mindedness and disciplined concentration on a carefully defined and rigidly mapped-out scope—cricketers and the ways of cricket—ensures that the writer and his personal world, not to mention the personal worlds of the people he describes, remain guarded and more or less out of bounds. In this way, Benaud in his writing, if not so much in his day-to-day life, is intriguingly reclusive.

If there was one area where Richie Benaud did not scrupulously observe his self-imposed avoidance of insider revelation, it was in writing about cricket administration and individual administrators. The unusual, almost incautious, intensity with which he sets about flaying the worst of the foolishness, unkindness, unearned privilege and pretentiousness of certain members of cricket's governing bodies during his playing years and later is refreshing, entertaining and, given the even tenor of his characteristic narrative and expository style, on the face of it, surprising. But you quickly realise that you shouldn't be surprised. Sturdy resistance to arrant silliness and pomposity is as characteristic of him as the personal boundaries he sets and meticulously observes in the general run of his writing.

As the English selectors began considering the team they would send to Australia for the 1958–59 Ashes tour, their deliberations were distinguished more by recrimination, squabbling and disagreement than by reason and logic. Benaud was well aware of this administrative 'dog's breakfast', as he called it, but only some time later would he realise that the equivalent Australian meetings and discussions were similarly combative and indecisive, and would also influence his own future and career in ways he could not possibly have foreseen or expected. Moreover, much of this debate was taking place behind closed doors.

Though Benaud did not suspect that some of the arguing was about him, it was easy to guess that his close friend Neil Harvey was a central concern of cricket administration in New South Wales. Returning just about broke from the South African tour, Harvey stood to earn £375 plus £50 expenses from the impending Test series against England. Harvey publicly announced that financial pressures might force him to leave Australia.

It was, as Benaud recognised and firmly pointed out, an appalling comment on the Australian Cricket Board that its best batsman—a star of the Invincibles a decade earlier and an automatic Test match selection since—was in danger of being forced out of the game because of financial pressures. The board was unmoved, and the standard rate of payment, £75 per Test and £10 expenses, remained unchanged. It is anecdotes like this one, and there are plenty of them, that make comprehensible the passion and fury of the players involved.

Anyone who has paid close attention to Australian cricket and its development over the past forty years or so is immediately reminded, as Benaud was in his stinging criticism of the Australian Cricket Board, of the player-payment negotiations in 1974–75. Record gate-takings had seemed to justify a pay rise for players, but the board had refused to co-operate. When Rod Marsh raised this issue with the board's administrator, Alan Barnes, a dressing-room gathering of Australian cricketers was told that there were fifty thousand others who would be prepared to play for Australia 'for nothing'.

Ian Chappell recalled that this infamous rejoinder prompted the Victorian and Australian opening batsman Ian Redpath, a quietly spoken, peaceable character, to grab Barnes by the throat, crush him up against the wall and yell in his face, 'You bloody idiot. Of course there are fifty thousand out there who would play for nothing. But how bloody good would the Australian team be?'

Benaud shared Redpath's anger, noting not only that Barnes's infamous statement was constantly resurrected in the press and elsewhere but also that the board, as if proud of the sentiment, quoted it, or versions of it, in private to players as if to ensure they toed the company line. The board's deliberate publication of the details of players' earnings in 1997 was, in Benaud's view, simply one more shameful episode in the same seedy drama designed to shape the public's view of elite cricketers as rich men not in need of any further privilege.

In *My Spin on Cricket*, Benaud devotes a whole chapter to the administrators, beginning with the veto placed on the selection of Sid Barnes in the aftermath of the Invincibles tour of England in 1948, which he deems a travesty. The controversy involved the faking of minutes, incredibly unwieldy selection processes, deliberate obfuscation and a libel case brought by Barnes against a member of the public. In Benaud's opinion the board's performance rivalled the farce and comic invention of 'Gilbert and Sullivan at their very best'. Judicial opinion re-enforced this description more soberly, representing the board's performance as chaotic, bigoted and, from a public relations point of view, disastrous.

Apart from specific examples of maladministration, misjudgement and unfairness that he relentlessly exposes when possible and relevant, a consistent theme of Benaud's criticism of the board's behaviour and decisions had been the disjunction of its members from the game and the sporting world they were seeking to control and direct, and he rarely misses a chance to puncture the afflatus of the self-important.

He portrays the board members and, with some honourable exceptions, cricket officialdom generally, as above all full of an entirely undeserved sense of entitlement and superiority 'in their navy blue suits, white shirts and strong leather shoes', not so subtly demanding reverential treatment. This emphasis on the sartorial splendour of the board members—especially the 'strong leather shoes', a wonderfully ironic touch—was a ploy Benaud used several times to portray how removed the board was from its players.

After the euphoria of the Tied Test, the Queensland Cricket Association complained that players had lingered too long in the dressing rooms. Benaud scathingly records the board's reaction to this complaint as wholehearted agreement:

> eleven of the twelve of them around the rich-red mahogany table enthusiastically outvoted Bradman's solitary dissension. Apart from Bradman, there may have been someone else present who had been in a dressing-room as a first-class player, but they were thin on the ground. The remainder knew little of what happened on a first-class cricket field, and they knew nothing at all of the camaraderie which existed

between players and opponents. Nor, I suspect, did they care over-much.

Again, the 'rich-red mahogany table' is—like the 'strong leather shoes'—the acutely observed and damning detail, the symbol of the officials' fatal disjunction from the players' world. Benaud's concern and emphasis is prescient because it was just this disjunction, along with the lofty and insensitive official attitude to player payment, that featured so largely in the grievances of the so-called Packer rebels, years later.

In *Anything But...An Autobiography*, Benaud records that Sir Donald Bradman was having a busy time at the start of the 1960s as chairman of the board, but he was clearly encouraged by 'the manner in which [Bradman] had approached his first year'. There would be even greater encouragement and reassurance, he adds, 'if, in future years, more ex-players made it on to the Board and into the Chairmanship'.

In *My Spin on Cricket*, after devoting forensic attention to the Sid Barnes fiasco, Benaud is happy to report great progress over the decades. 'Cricket Australia have done a great job in Australian cricket in recent years; ex-players have been brought in to help administer the game, and there is good rapport between administrators and players.' By 2005, knowledge of how to run the sport was balanced with awareness of what it's like to be on the field of play.

Benaud's books are full of judicious opinion, attractive reminiscence, robust argumentation, wonderful anecdotes and, perhaps most importantly, genuinely riveting, dramatic descriptions of some great games of cricket. Although it is not always obvious, because much of the narrative is constrained by noted fact and memory, his books, from the splendid *A Tale of Two Tests* onwards, are the work of a writer. The writerly signs are present sometimes fleetingly, often with an almost throw-away casual air, at other times with real flair.

The whole performance, like his television commentary, is subject to careful controls of tone, rhythm and balance. That *A Tale of Two Tests* might be the best of them, despite the greater maturity and confidence of the later works, suggests that he had a knack and a feeling for the imaginative, atmospheric and dramatic without sacrificing his own preference for the more documentary style of narrative.

Benaud begins the acknowledgments in what would be his final book, *Over But Not Out: My Life So Far*, by explaining that, after *Anything But…An Autobiography* was published in 1998, he and Daphne, his collaborator on so many books, had decided not to add to the Benaud oeuvre. But he points out that the ensuing six years were so eventful in the cricket world that *My Spin on Cricket* fulfilled the need to catch up in 2005. *Over But Not Out* followed five years later. It reproduces the whole text of *Anything But…An Autobiography* with the addition of a number of wide-ranging chapters and six equally eclectic appendices.

Chapter 31 of *Anything But…An Autobiography*, which is entitled 'A Sad Farewell', becomes Chapter 44 of *Over But Not Out* and whereas the original 'A Sad Farewell' relates the circumstances of Lou Benaud's death, the sad farewell of *Over But Not Out* is a salute to his mother, who died aged 104. The final chapter of *Anything But...An Autobiography*, 'The Benaud Connection', becomes Chapter 31 of *Over But Not Out*. There is absolutely nothing wrong with this procedure. Benaud, in collaboration with his publisher, is entirely at liberty to turn again to his earlier material, and the repetition endows *Over But Not Out*—a book which, given his earlier assurance to Daphne, really was his last—with something of the quality of a collected works, in the manner of the poets.

This is another aspect of Benaud's control. He returns to and recreates his favoured milieu and his most potent scenes, recollections and ideas much as a fiction writer or a composer, loath to abandon a golden seam, reworks or plays variations on themes that have already surfaced imaginatively but are too potent, haunting, illuminating or serious to discard. And in doing so, the writer or the composer tightens control over the original inspiration and the texture of the idea, and takes new varieties of momentum from it.

A true Francophile in his later years, Benaud took some delight in his memory of the village bearing his name along the D229 from Clermont-Ferrand. But despite that fortunate coincidence, the hamlet of Benaud offers nothing more personal or revealing about its namesake. The works of Richie Benaud, the writer, are something like that. The literary road to Benaud will take you through plenty of cricket, and all the territory, atmosphere, routines, characters and drama that surround the game, but it won't reveal a great deal about the Benaud behind it all. Such personal revelations exist, but they are rare, carefully deployed and strictly controlled. Still, it is a road of events, colour, and majestic and quixotic exploits, a full panoply of characters, human complexity, dignity and interest. In short, a journey eminently worth making.

11

CHANNEL NINE DAYS

Our Richie, Colossus of Cool

'Often, though I had seen every ball bowled in a match,
I came to understand what had happened and why only
after viewing the highlights the next day on TV. Nonetheless,
there remain compelling reasons for preferring the holistic
sprawl of cricket in the flesh to the fragmented but highly
focused experience of cricket on television.'
MIKE MARQUSEE, *War Minus the Shooting*

Richie Benaud was criticised at times by various pundits for not being as involved in cricket administration as someone of his experience, knowledge and influence might have been. Unlike Sir Donald Bradman, for example, he was never a selector nor, indeed, an administrator of any official kind. As Gideon Haigh observed, 'At times, one would have wished for more from Benaud—the occasional trenchant judgement or firm moral stand.' Bill Lawry, unwilling to criticise his former captain and long-time friend, nevertheless agreed. Benaud, he writes, had 'one of the most brilliant cricket brains in the world and, on reflection, cricket has suffered from the fact that [he] has never taken on an administrative position in world cricket, apart from [the part he played] in the success of World Series Cricket'.

Probably the truth is that Benaud didn't need official positions. His presence in the world of cricket, through his television commentary in England and then on Channel Nine in Australia, was pervasive, deeply respected and, by and large, influential. And he did enter into the field of judgment and take firm stands in his books. It is just that, reasonably popular and often very good though they are, his books have not reached anything like the audience he commanded on television, and in those commentaries he was renowned not for cutting judgments and firm moral stands, but for cool and magisterial reticence. His silences or brevities could be full of implication or simply assuaging.

Whatever the case, the fleeting ironies, brilliantly caught moments of excitement and the capacity to communicate the profundity of cricket's sui generis character—possibly because Benaud himself was sui generis—in the Benaud commentary conveyed without self-consciousness the very essence of cricket's eccentricity as well as its thoroughgoing normality, its capacity to unfold the most unlooked-for scripts: to be in his words 'the most controversial game of all', or to settle, apparently, into comfortable predictability.

When Benaud joined Kerry Packer's so-called cricket revolution, bringing not only his extraordinary resources of experience, knowledge and understanding as a player and commentator, but also, as Gideon Haigh puts it, lending it 'a patina of respectability', he became a part of Channel Nine cricket. Though needless to say he never commented publicly on the programming, he was undoubtedly aware of, and advised Packer and Channel Nine on, the ways in which televised cricket, having passed from the sure but staid ABC to commercialism's Wide World of Sports, would need to improve.

In its first years at least, Channel Nine's version was subject to and invited satire from various quarters, and only the incomparable Richie Benaud was spared. Back in the early 1980s, for example, when the Central Commentary Position team was made up of Bill Lawry, Tony Greig, Ian Chappell, and off and on Keith Stackpole and Max Walker, all under the benign, unruffled orchestration of Benaud, writing for the *Adelaide Review* I saw it like this:

> In the beginning are the commercials. Also at the start and finish of each over, during drinks, at the fall of a wicket, while occasional technical hitches are repaired, and as a consolation if it rains...Your head becomes stuffed with visuals and jingles; and you are overrun by avalanches of advertisements into which fleeting subliminalities of cricket have been skilfully flickered with such austere frequency as will just satisfy the vestigial and tattered requirements of the Trades Descriptions Act.
>
> These days [1985] Channel Nine has perfected the art of turning cricket into more or less one long

advertisement. That car, for example, which the International Cricketer of the Year wins, used to be propped on a dais down near the sightscreen…and was occasionally featured. But this season it's become the subject of a regular car ad running right through an over…

A day's cricket on Channel Nine starts with a few affabilities from Richie Benaud, a brace or two of advertisements, and then it's over to Tony Greig in the middle for another in his series of hilarious encounters with technology. Here we learn about 'Player comfort levels' ('Are you comfortable?' says Border to Gooch. 'It's a living, Alan, it's a living'); or what Tony calls the 'wund' velocity. Although you can measure the strength of the 'wund', the penetrability of the 'putch' defies technology and can only be assessed by the insertion of Tony's car keys, proving that cricket is not succumbing wholly to the 'glutter' of the age.

Unfair no doubt, embellishing, ignoring or slanting the truth of things—just as Billy Birmingham's 'Twelfth Man' series did with the accents, foibles and voices of the commentary team. Without sponsors and their advertisements, there would be no cricket but, as Tony Lewis observed, in a comment quoted by Benaud in *My Spin on Cricket*, 'along the way the beautiful game has needed protecting.'

In its earliest manifestations, cricket on Channel Nine was, in the view of some, in thrall to commercialism and not sufficiently protected. As far as the actual commentary was concerned, it's difficult not to wonder whether Benaud, with his impeccable performance and rigorous training by consummate professionals, ever despaired in those early days at the amateurism of some of his colleagues, at their dogged refusal to concede to his view that the commentary box required constant and intense concentration. Above all, as Benaud reiterates in different books and articles, the viewer can see the same picture as the commentator, so that any words spoken must add to that picture, not parrot or simply footnote it, and this is a difficult art to master.

Benaud several times and in various forums questioned the mystique of the commentator. In his view, the proposition that the commentator was the crucial and most important ingredient in the broadcast could hardly have been further from the truth. The commentator's task and responsibility was to add to what was on the screen quietly, noisily, subtly, dogmatically or generously—whatever mode best suited his or her personality.

This concession to the many possible differing styles of sports commentators is a reminder of Benaud's own broad experience, beginning with his days observing and training under the mentorship of Tom Sloan. But acknowledgment of the range of individuality does not bring with it a tolerance of self-indulgence, and there was a good deal of that among his colleagues in Channel Nine's early years. As I wrote about commentators and their ways in the 1980s:

Only Richie Benaud, who is an incomparably good commentator, and Ian Chappell, who is nearly as good as long as he resists the temptation to reminisce, believe that the viewing audience can actually see what's happening via the miracle of television; the others tell you every move—'It's in the air, Tufnell's getting under it, oh no, he's dropped it!' screams Bill ('It's all happening') Lawry. 'Yes, Bill, that one went high in the air, Tufnell got well under it and then spilt it,' says Keith ('Stacky') Stackpole, wrapping it up. Lawry, a tremendously amiable and often very perceptive commentator, sometimes becomes the victim of his own genuine and engaging enthusiasm and enjoys a good shout. And then there is Max Walker, who wages a spectacular, non-stop campaign to abolish not only silence but also all conjunctions and sequence from the English language: 'Pressure building up; good line; Melbourne Arts Centre in the background; adrenalin flowing; seagulls a bit flighty out there; wrapping the fingers round the cherry; good light; Botanic Gardens very colourful; caressing the seam...'

The tensions and acrimonies, personal loyalties and disloyalties that had distinguished the Packer coup tended to sharpen the commentary team's initial sense of being under siege, but the strength of feeling that informed the often bitter sentiments of people like Ian Chappell, Dennis Lillee and other World

Series cricketers had its roots far back in Test cricket history. When Kerry Packer made his clarion call, years of patronising, penny-pinching and mean-minded treatment of Australia's international cricketers—the kind of administrative attitudes and slights that Richie Benaud tirelessly exposed and attacked in his books—had come to a head. At last there was a way out of the Board of Control hegemony and, with Packer's powerful support, Benaud's cool guidance and Ian Chappell's truculent espousal, the uprising was launched and executed.

Just how embattled the Channel Nine team and its sponsors and backers really were is difficult to assess all these years later. At the time they represented themselves as grievously but bravely isolated, and this condition became the raison d'être of *Ten Turbulent Years* (1987), one of the early publications announcing the success of the commercial uprising. But like so much that was written, claimed and argued at that time, before peace was declared and the division between the Packer camp and the traditionalists was healed forever, *Ten Turbulent Years* was mostly propaganda, history written by the winners.

According to its blurb, it was 'a lively, no-punches-pulled account of the most tempestuous decade in Australian cricket history'. In truth, however, it was about as turbulent as sump oil, stuffed full of verbiage, gossip, posturing, limp pseudo-confrontation and passing attacks of righteousness without much pretence to form, purpose or order. None of this was very surprising. It's difficult to be tempestuous and punchy when you are spending all your time admiring yourself in the mirror. *Ten*

Turbulent Years was so keen on itself that Narcissus, had he been around, could have taken its correspondence course.

In the chummy, self-regarding world of *Ten Turbulent Years* the villains were all those who originally expressed, or who came around to expressing, the slightest disagreement with or misgiving about the 'cricket revolution'; and 'cricket revolution' meant, for the purposes of this book, One Day cricket, in particular with what had come to be recognised as its characteristic Channel Nine trappings—abundant advertising, coloured clothing, catchphrases and slogans, and so on. Those villains who dared to dissent were, apparently, upper-class twits, cut off from the real world, suspiciously Anglophile, scarcely real Aussies at all. So, for example, in his contribution, 'Glory, Then the Revolution', Tony Lewis, an ex-cricketer and cricket writer, asks what better time could there have been 'to stir a revolution' than in the aftermath of the sensational Centenary Test at the MCG in 1977: 'The rulers were relaxed partying, and believing with every draught of Armagnac that the good times were with them forever.' In case we miss the point, Lewis refers to the players a line or two later as 'workers or entertainers, call them what you will...'

Ian Wooldridge, in his piece called 'Cricket Goes to Court', uses the same storm-the-barricades parlance in his account of the Packer World Series Cricket court case: 'Stubbornly the opposition [i.e. cricket traditionalists] refused to capitulate. It was convinced that God and the Establishment—most members of the British Establishment acknowledge no difference between the two—must prevail.' The fact was, Wooldridge continues, that 'World Series Cricket, or some such revolutionary institution, was always going to happen…You cannot forever…expect forelock-tugging subservience.' Dennis Lillee, in 'Cricket Sees the Light', adopts a similar off-with-their-heads tone: 'Cricket was never going to be the same, who'd ever heard of cricketers wearing anything but white…playing with a white ball… playing at night? No wonder the Establishment purists damn near choked on their pink gins!'

Channel Nine's David Hill, in 'Putting You in the Picture', describes the 'howls of anguish' that he says greeted Channel Nine's new technological cricket coverage,

> making a mockery of the game…Retired Colonels wrote huffing letters about never watching Channel Nine again…Retired cricketers demanded such and such a commentator be replaced because, although he may have represented Australia for umpteen Tests, it was obvious to the writer who had played D grade for the last thirty years that so-and-so knew nothing about the game.

And so it went. In short, here's how the *Ten Turbulent Years* game changers saw you if you were not beside yourself about 'revolutionary' entrepreneurial cricket and its media mentor, Channel Nine. You were elderly to frankly old ('retired'); pompous, ridiculous ('colonel'); presuming superiority (expecting 'forelock tugging subservience'); irrational and resistant to change ('huffing letters'); a member of an elite, affluent group (drinking Armagnac or pink gin, unlike the ordinary bloke with his Fosters or Fourex); an unskilled, cricketing nonentity ('played D grade for the last thirty years'). These are the straw men so fearlessly shafted in the unturbulent pages of *Ten Turbulent Years*.

The other side of this coin is the self-congratulation: the indomitability of Kerry Packer, the amazing innovativeness of Channel Nine, Channel Nine's risk-taking, the determined endurance of Channel Nine against the 'howls' of the 'purists', the makeshift days of World Series Cricket, the gradual triumph of World Series Cricket, the courage of those who, to quote Phil Wilkins (from his 'In the Footsteps of Heroes'), 'stood in the firing line of the arch-conservative forces of moderation and establishment stagnation'. Essay after essay—by bludgeoning, repetition, innuendo or aside—hammers home the message: New Cricket Good, Old Cricket Bad.

Nowhere in *Ten Turbulent Years* is there any analysis of the clash of principle and ideology that the cricket rebellion involved. Nowhere does anyone attempt to understand and explain the personal hurts, feuds, animosities and career crises that the rupture engendered. Nowhere is there allowed to surface even a vestige of a suspicion that any decisions taken in the remaking of cricket might have been—well—wrong.

But there were those who walked the tightrope without contemplating the safety net of rampant triumphalism or conceding their own integrity. Alan McGilvray was one of these. His fine piece, guardedly entitled 'Speaking of Cricket', says much by implication. Allan Border's essay on the importance of the Sheffield Shield competition is thoughtful and necessary. And Richie Benaud, who with ten years of Channel Nine commentary experience behind him and with a promising future opening up for the ever more expert technological coverage of cricket is, as always, balanced, judicious and eloquent when he chooses to be but at some points a master of the calculated silence, just as he was in the commentary box.

Ten Turbulent Years is long gone, as it should be, but it was an important moment for Benaud. As the mastermind of the Packer assault, he had certainly not been an éminence grise, but somehow he maintained an appearance of reasonable detachment. To an important extent, this was brought about by his commentary style. He was always well informed, quite restrained but full of well-turned praise when it was warranted and equally capable of stern critical appraisal when necessary. The contained fury of his signing off after the underarm ball was only one of many occasions when his viewers could feel assured of the absolute integrity of his views and the profound sincerity with which he expressed them, all untarnished by excessive emotional show or self-regarding demonstrativeness.

Benaud achieved the difficult feat of being a Packer man while continuing to be his own man and, as the heat, divisiveness and personal animosities of the 'cricket revolution' gradually abated, he emerged more and more impressively as leader, tactician, and centre of gravity and gravitas. The former Australian fast bowler Brett Lee said, 'When Richie walks into the Channel Nine box everyone stands up. When Richie was on air, you'd see all the commentators listening in to see what he had to say.' Strangely, however, Benaud's superlative example—in manner, meticulous preparation, delivery, range of cricketing reference, self-discipline—seems not to have passed into the collective mien of the Channel Nine commentary team over the decades of its dominance of televised cricket.

The critiques of Channel Nine cricket quoted here are from the 1980s, relatively early days in the life of the commentary box. In thirty years or so, however, a gradual change in personnel has produced only marginal differences in style and presentation, and the coverage seems to have attracted much the same criticisms and expressions of dissatisfaction. In 2015 the *Guardian*'s Geoff Lemon offered a lengthy, blistering assessment of the state of play.

> Something weird happened during India's recent Test tour of Australia. On television sets across a nation, not just once but over and over.
>
> Michael Clarke talked about the cricket.
>
> In slightly shy, broadcast-unsteady tones, Australia's then-injured captain analysed why Chris Rogers had edged a ball, how Shane Watson used the seam, why David Warner had two gullies, how Virat Kohli worked opposing fieldsmen, when Steve Smith would declare.

Between times, the regular cast of Nine's Wide World of Sports held important discourse about the Commonwealth Bank and what a good bloke Glenn McGrath is and how every Australian cricket ground is really great.

This was pretty tough stuff but, as I recall—having been glued to the screen through that and subsequent sessions—it's a fairly accurate reconstruction. Lemon quotes a viewer whose poor vision meant he relied heavily on the audio commentary and who records that he enjoyed 'Clarke and his insights *when he is allowed to express them*' (my italics). 'Let's be honest,' Lemon says:

Nine's cricket coverage has never been a place where genius came to joust. Unchaperoned, though, recent seasons have subsided into a swamp of hokey back-slapping. Grown men call each other Tubby and Binga and Slats, not as nicknames but a full-time mode of address. The guffaw is king. It's all about being the matiest mates who ever mated.

Lemon then turns his blowtorch on Michael Slater and especially James Brayshaw, before portraying Mike Hussey as 'perched quietly to one side' and Mark Nicholas, 'a fine writer on the game', as similarly marginalised, 'like a school-play carica-ture of a nobleman stranded in the colonies, unable to hedge or redirect'.

This relentless, uncompromising severity continues as Lemon warms to his theme. Two moments are especially interesting. Unmistakably, the 'chaperone' Lemon has in mind is Benaud and the implication, equally clearly, is that he kept the commentary team under control, that he exercised a spoken or, more likely, an assumed authority, which enjoined on his colleagues standards not only of actual commentary, but also of general presence and demeanour. There was a way of behaving when you were in the commentary box, whether on air or not, which Lemon credibly implies was the Benaud way and which, by and large, his colleagues observed. With Benaud gone, and some new blood introduced, this mostly unspoken authority quickly lapsed.

The second moment is the reference to Mark Nicholas. As Benaud's presence and commanding role in Channel Nine cricket commentary gradually—and necessarily—diminished, Nicholas became the ever more likely successor after the Wide World of Sports indulged a brief, apparent flirtation with Mark Taylor as a possible leader.

Nicholas, often cited as the best English cricketer of his time never to play a Test match, had a distinguished career in County Cricket, playing for and captaining Hampshire on a number of successful campaigns. Eloquent and educated, he came to Channel Nine with considerable broadcasting and television experience and reputation following his retirement from first-class cricket. Although he matches Benaud's urbanity, has a comparable range of cricket reference and memory, and is impressively comfortable and in charge as the anchor of the commentary box, he is nevertheless a very different proposition.

Although he rarely engages in Bill Lawry-style shouts of joy, admiration, catastrophe or disgust, he can still transmit his own excitement and attractive, almost boyish, anticipatory pleasure at the cricket he and the viewers are about to enjoy. He does not have, nor does he aspire to, the Benaud style of calm detachment, but he is measured and considering in his narrative and judgments. He is not imperturbable and doesn't seek to be, but he is the calm centre of the commentary box by virtue of training, temperament, personal magnetism and good humour. Lemon's characterisation of him as a 'school-play caricature of a nobleman stranded in the colonies, unable to hedge or redirect' is unfair, inaccurate, and probably a case of Lemon's attack taking him further than he designed while maintaining a tone and an intensity that he certainly did design.

These two moments are integral to a metamorphosis of Channel Nine cricket: the loss of the 'chaperone' removed the powerful unifying, fashioning force of Benaud's skill and high expectations. Nicholas inherited a different group, in which a strong larrikin streak flourished free of the Benaud shadow and no longer mindful of the Benaud commentating example. In a sense, the swiftness and completeness with which the tight Benaud model disintegrated is a further tribute to the magnetic force of the Benaud centre around which these satellites had revolved. And it was not Nicholas's fault that the planetary system began to wobble. When Benaud more or less retired, and especially when he was injured and became ill, the system's sun went out.

Lemon is right to see Channel Nine cricket as now 'part commentary, part cheer squad' as a result of the composition of the commentating group, and to note a deterioration of professionalism. The latter is partly indicated by what he calls the 'national embarrassment' of 'a yawning ignorance about the opposition, piped to millions of fans through networks around the world'.

Even in the relatively slapdash early days of Tony Grieg, Bill Lawry, Max Walker, Keith Stackpole and others, there was at least a discernible degree of preparation. Respect for the game of cricket has been the casualty: there is a 'new regime', of which James Brayshaw is the 'forward marker'. It is not just the absence of the kind of preparation for which Benaud was renowned, and to which Nicholas and Chappell also pay serious and continued attention. It is a kind of pride in parading ignorance, a 'deliberate idiocy'. As Lemon puts it, 'not just not knowing, but making a point of not knowing, and of telling us he doesn't know'.

The television audience is being encouraged to pay little attention to the opposing teams, about whom it seems, as far as the commentators are concerned, not much is known, and to concentrate on the Aussies. 'Jingoism is now Nine's province,' Lemon argues. 'Too many links to the administration and players mean that cricket is called by company men. That's literal for Cricket Australia board member [Mark] Taylor, and recent Big

Bash players [Brett] Lee and [Michael] Hussey. The rest know which side their party pies are sauced.'

Again, this is unremittingly harsh, but not far below the jagged surface is a current of uncomfortable truth. The ignorance, the insidiousness of an infiltration of company men, and the apparently total lack of interest in anything but the margins of the local game are all points well taken. The distance the coverage has travelled from the Benaud days in such a short time is startling until one recognises—again—that in the 'information age' opinions, ideas, fads, emphases, obsessions and insights all travel fluidly not just through the months or years but through the hours and minutes and on into oblivion until some signal, reference, need or accident resurrects them.

Richie Benaud was already fading from sight, and from sound, when he began his protracted stepping back from the Channel Nine forefront. When he was hurt in a car crash and incapacitated, his presence dwindled further to a few television clips. Channel Nine floated the possibility that he would do some commentary from his lounge-room chair. Fortunately, good sense prevailed.

Benaud's death, sadly, brought that familiar figure, face and voice back into our consciousness and memory again, but it won't be for long. Though his fame and reputation will endure, as they certainly should, he is already fading from the everyday. Life plunges on. In the Channel Nine commentary box his spirit wanes and his example is gradually lost.

One survivor, however, through the many iterations of

Channel Nine cricket—the last man standing of the originals now that Bill Lawry has stepped away from the microphone—is the craggy, pugnacious, though mellowing Ian Chappell. He was close to Benaud during the World Series Cricket upheavals, and then in the commentary box and socially.

In conversation with Ashley Mallett, Chappell said, 'Richie's advice has always been to the point and full of common sense. Whether it is business or cricket or life in general, he is the person I turn to.' Their cricketing paths crossed in 1962 when, as Chappell recalled it, 'South Australia had just enjoyed a rare victory over a star-studded New South Wales line-up. Benaud, as the not-out batsman, magnanimously stood back to allow Les Favell's team to walk off the Adelaide Oval first. I was on the field as twelfth man and wasn't about to leave ahead of the Australian captain and a man whose leadership style I'd admired from afar, but he insisted.

'That story is indicative of Benaud,' Chappell concluded. 'He was a thorough gentleman and meticulous in his preparation—I was staggered he knew my name.' In the next year, Chappell scored his maiden first-class century at the Adelaide Oval— again the opponent was Benaud's powerful New South Wales side—before travelling to England to play Lancashire League for Ramsbottom. When he arrived at his new club, he found a new Gray-Nicolls bat waiting for him, compliments of Richie Benaud.

Chappell, as player, as South Australian and Australian captain, truculent campaigner for the rights and rewards of cricketers, obdurate critic of what he judged to be Bradman's penny-pinching attitude to player payment, and World Series Cricket leader on and off the field, was intellectually sharp and enquiring, impatient of convention, suspicious of authority that found its justification only in tradition, and open to daring, even revolutionary decisions and solutions. In Benaud he found and admired what he described as 'a mind that was regularly in lateral thinking mode'.

Of all the ex-players who Benaud blooded for Channel Nine's commentary team, Chappell was the most likely to follow his example because he understood more clearly than the others the nature of that example, even if, in his own early commentating days, he found emulation difficult for one reason or another. Recognising this, Geoff Lemon notes that 'only Chappell remained, the least subtle of the old regime becoming an unlikely bastion of broadcasting excellence in the new.'

If Ian Chappell is the temporary custodian of the Benaud commentating legacy, then it is no doubt in good hands, but where are the other candidates? Are they so rare because Benaud was inimitable? Canvassing the commentariat, the cricket writer and academic Rob Steen determined that the finest practitioners among them sell subtlety. 'They are thoughtful, unhurried cheer-leaders. They don't rush to judgment, reach for the hype pills or let local bias defeat professional neutrality. They rise above the din. They also know how to anticipate, detect and analyse the catalytic moments, and to articulate our own responses.' Steen says the best commentators are, like the rest of us, the army of cricket nuts and appreciative fans, the key difference being that, by and large, their critiques stem from first-hand experience, albeit ever more distant.

'No cricketing honour can match the Richie Benaud Seal of Approval...Our Richie, the Caliph of Cool, the Imam of Implacability, would walk into any commentary team anywhere, anytime, be it the West Sussex Tiddlywinks Championship or a sultan's wedding. No one, as John Lennon once boasted, is in his tree.'

Well, Our Richie has gone and, at Australian grounds at least, Ian Chappell and Mark Nicholas seem to be the only credible candidates to claim his mantle. Shane Warne, with his sharp cricket brain and astute grasp of the subtleties of the game, could aspire to that class, but he cannot always be trusted to 'rise above the din' which, by and large, is provided by the others in the Channel Nine box, who are, to borrow Steen's description, commentators as showmen as distinct from commentators as narrators.

It is hard to resist the kind of flourish that Benaud spurned in his books and in his commentary. He was the nonpareil—matchless and incomparable—sailing with supreme dominion through the world of cricket which he adorned, loved and made his own.

12

RICHIE BENAUD

Bowling, Bowling, Bowling

'The spontaneous outburst of thousands at a fierce hook or a
dazzling slip-catch, the ripple of recognition at a long-awaited
leg-glance, are as genuine and deeply felt expressions of
artistic emotion as any I know.' C. L. R. JAMES

The distinguished cricket writer and music critic Neville Cardus
recounts in his autobiography a vivid but slightly odd memory of
the outbreak of World War II.

> On the Friday morning when Hitler invaded Poland,
> I chanced to be in the Long Room at Lord's...As I
> watched the ghostly movements of the players outside,
> a beautifully preserved member of Lord's, spats and
> rolled umbrella, stood near me inspecting the game...
> Suddenly two workmen entered the Long Room in
> green aprons and carrying a bag. They took down the

bust of W. G. Grace, put it into the bag and departed with it. The noble lord at my side watched their every movement; then he turned to me. 'Did you see, sir?' he asked. I told him I had seen. 'This means war,' he said.

Richie Benaud would have understood and enjoyed that incident because his reverence for the game of cricket and commitment to it was of the same order, if not as comically catastrophic, as that of the gentleman of Lord's. With C. L. R. James he would have agreed that the experience of cricket at its best, whether you are playing or watching, is an experience of art. Just as so many remain in thrall to the great books, or the finest paintings or the films of the ages, so Richie Benaud was captivated by Annie Proulx's wonderful novel *The Shipping News*, and the voices of Bocelli and Brightman, and the mysterious chiaroscuro of an evening French landscape, but he never wearied of cricket—playing it, writing about it, discussing it, noting, tracing and evaluating its endless variety.

Like Neville Cardus, he brought to his love of cricket and his representations of it, whether at the microphone or in print, an extraordinarily open mind and a quietly voracious desire to experience the game's every shade, nuance, drama, sensation, surprise. The doctrinaire rigidities and bondage to tradition implied by the 'noble lord's' spats and rolled umbrella were never a part of Benaud's 'spin on cricket'.

On the contrary, the ease with which he accepted developments that looked to the eyes of aficionados, at the time of their unveiling, outlandish and destructive to the spirit and dignity of the game, surprised even his most devoted supporters. Far from feeling protective, Benaud seemed full of curiosity about what the ancient game might come up with next. As he often demonstrated on the field, in the heat of play, and later in argument and discussion, he was not afraid of change or experiment, and he was philosophical when innovation or risk didn't succeed. He mostly took pleasure in change, even novelty.

To the opponents of Twenty20 cricket, he pointed out that a brand of cricket attractive to massive numbers of spectators and televised around the world to millions could not, at least in the long run, be bad for the game. Though he didn't live to see the long run, his bland confidence gave waverers and enthusiasts alike a sense of security about an initially insidious phenomenon. Benaud considered that, just as One Day cricket had provided a template and justification for change by demonstrably sharpening stroke play, running between wickets, fielding and decision-making, challenging captaincy in new and lateral ways, so Twenty20 would make its own individual and eccentric contributions to the good of the game. But he conceded that not all players would be able to manage Twenty20's mixture of freneticism, improvisation and precision.

As usual he proposed a tantalising embellishment, recognising that many cricketers who will never be selected in a Test side play the One Day and Twenty20 versions with great skill and panache. Winning the Twenty20 World Cup and the One Day World Cup, Benaud proposed, should become the ambition of all cricketers below Test rank. These are typical Richie Benaud leaps: a provocative but not shocking view, full of good sense and acceptance of risk. And it had the innovator's blithe disregard for minor, manageable difficulties. Benaud had, after all, steered the cricket world into and through the 'Packer revolution' with the same mixture of steely resolve, problem-solving acumen and unobtrusive flair.

Appendix V to *Over But Not Out*, appearing as it does near the end of what Benaud himself, and Daphne, recognised would be his last full-length book, has a certain benign yet pointed score-settling character. There is one last acerbic glance at the front-foot no-ball, Benaud's bête noir since its introduction (and Bradman's too, for the record), headed, 'An interesting statistic on no-balls in Test Cricket'. Comparing statistics on the number of Test cricket no-balls under the back-foot rule between 1876–77 and 1968–69, during which there were fewer than five thousand, with the thirty thousand no-balls bowled in Test cricket under the front-foot rule from 1969–70 to 2010, he asks—and you can see in imagination that look of quizzical irony that accompanies the question—what can possibly be the grounding of common sense in the front-foot rule, an English invention?

Benaud makes it seem self-evident, and to many it is, but his old and valued team mate Bob Simpson was one of several past and present players who disagreed. The law was introduced to curtail fast bowlers' 'drag' but, Simpson explained, with a nicely mischievous touch, 'most bowlers, including Richie, were draggers and this allowed them to get even closer to the batsmen before they let the ball go.' As an opening batsman, Simpson had vivid and unpleasant memories of drag 'from which fast bowlers [derived] a huge advantage…and the rule was changed to force all bowlers to deliver the ball from the appropriate distance.'

Benaud's final sally in this appendix, which he delivers with unmistakable irony given his intermittent criticisms of cricket officialdom, concerns the colour of the ball, which he considers an interesting matter for administrators to 'ponder'. Multi-coloured exaggeration signifies his exasperation with this, as he sees it, non-problem, one which he had already explored several times with assorted journalists. It is another example of Benaud encouraging the administration to use the handsome resources at their disposal for the good and advancement of the game.

He asks why so little financial support has been granted to studying ball colour in general and on producing an effective white ball in particular. With a typically lateral leap, he wonders what can be learned from the 2010 soccer World Cup's use of a white football in South Africa and, contrary to more or less universal acceptance of the 'two balls per innings innovation' in One Day cricket, he hints that more attentive research might have produced a better result.

The Packer takeover, coloured clothing, the white ball, the razzamatazz at the One Day Internationals reminiscent of the American way of sports, World Series Cricket and the great schism all had their hour, leaving trails of grave disturbance, dispute, excitement and upheaval from which Richie Benaud emerged not merely unscathed but undaunted, taking it all as it came, without expostulation, apparent anxiety or much objection. Caught on one occasion for a surprise quick interview by radio commentators who clearly wanted to pin him down on topics they assumed he would find problematic, he blindsided them completely by offering no objection to day–night Test matches—a proposition which, despite the successful Adelaide Oval Test in 2015, even liberal-minded fans continue to be uneasy about or thoroughly opposed to—and making his point about the ball, which for nocturnal Test matches would have to be highly sophisticated, one that would remain visible for many hours despite taking huge punishment.

And before his interlocutors could get another word in, he went on to suggest that modern science, particularly space-exploration technology, would surely come up with such an innovation if the scientists set their minds to it. On the back foot, the interviewers attempted to steer the conversation to Michael Clarke, whose controversial girlfriend at the time was Lara Bingle, a model and celebrity, but Benaud simply alerted them to his own beautiful girlfriend, his wife, Daphne, and left the discussion with his customary sangfroid undisturbed.

As Gideon Haigh observed, Benaud was not a controversialist. He could have been much more influential—as a selector, for example, as a revered and idolised ex-player, as one of the great captains and cricket brains. That he confined his sphere of influence to the commentary box and his published work and journalism was a posture which many, like Haigh, regretted.

It was, all things considered, a pity, but it was a thoroughly consistent position.

For all his public life, from his earliest days as an up-and-coming New South Wales cricketer to his last years, Benaud achieved that most difficult of personal compromises—maintaining a closely guarded private self without being or seeming to be reclusive. No one who had anything to do with him, even at some distance, like most of his admirers, could doubt, for example, that he adored Daphne, or that he loved to have a bet on the nags, or that he enjoyed a good, flinty Meursault, or that he rather idolised Keith Miller—and so on. But no one could own or claim him, as fans and acolytes are prone to do with their avatars.

They could own Shane Warne, who at the packed MCG would amiably acknowledge the hooligan chant of 'Waaarnie' and who would sometimes act on the field in ways that accorded with the mob's attitudes. And they once owned Dennis Lillee, beating time to his run-up, and Merv Hughes, whose warm-up exercises at deep fine leg were hilariously mimicked by hundreds of Merv Hugheses. Conversely, the members of that ever-growing group of cricket supporters in the stands known as the Richies, dressed and coiffed like him, and laughable in the best sense of the word partly because there are so many of them, are actually showing respect for their favourite cricketer at a courteous distance.

The 'Benaud' of Billy Birmingham's 'Twelfth Man' is very funny, but the humour depends on Birmingham's Benaud behaving in ways that we all know are exactly the opposite of how the real Benaud behaved and on his saying on air things that would be totally anathema to him. The humour is in that instantly recognisable voice—Birmingham is a brilliant mimic—giving itself away as fake with expletives, painful puns, and by being generally disgraceful. Birmingham's Benaud wants to be in control but can't manage it, partly because of the inadequacies of his colleagues and partly because of his own surrender to exasperation and impatience. In this manifestation, he is occasionally reminiscent of the hapless Dr Pym in the pre-war radio serial *Yes, What?* as he struggles to control Greenbottle, Bottomly, Standforth, Algernon de Pledge and, now and then, just to tighten the comparison, another (and very different!) Daphne.

In the commentary box, the real Benaud exercised control by example. Impeccably presented—the jackets metamorphosed into the famous beige over the years—thoroughly prepared, calm and composed but not, despite some characterisations of him, icy ('What a catch!'), Benaud became the voice of television cricket and the voice of summer, because he was mellifluous, authoritative and personal. Like Alan McGilvray on radio, he made you feel he was talking especially to you and not even the dissonance, silliness or intrusiveness of the advertising could upset this connection with the viewer, whereas, especially in the first decade or so at Channel Nine, some of his colleagues talked so ceaselessly and emptily that an advertisement or two was a relief.

His brilliant cricket gifts as batsman, fielder and, above all, bowler, and his often tightrope-walking captaincy, have been somewhat overwhelmed by his later eminence as Channel Nine's commentary leader and his cricket writing and journalism, but the power of his presence, what Mark Browning has rightly called his 'quiet charisma', reached that stage of pervasiveness that resulted in his name, image, reputation, accepted significance or associations being enlisted not only by satirists and mimics—some of whom, Benaud once drily observed, should return to their day jobs—but also by less likely admirers. One of these is the Benaud Trio.

'What's in a name?' asks Juliet in Shakespeare's tragedy *Romeo and Juliet* and answers her own question by suggesting: not much. 'That which we call a rose / By any other name would smell as sweet.' But when it comes to naming music groups, Sarah Grote, of the eccentrically named Stringents Quartet in Oklahoma, says:

> My best suggestion is to name your group something
> with a good story. People love the names of bands, and
> they are always going to ask, what's your story? How'd
> you come up with your name? So, I would say, look
> for a creative name, a strong, memorable name—but
> make sure it's a name with an interesting story.

The Benaud Trio—Amir Farid (piano), Lachlan Bramble (violin) and Ewen Bramble (cello)—would certainly please Sarah Grote with their choice of name, which is creative, strong and memorable, and their reasons for deciding on it. Unlike many of their fellow musicians, they rejected using the names of cities, as in the Tokyo String Quartet, the names of composers, as in the Borodin String Quartet, or famous instrument makers, as in the Stradivari Quartet, for example, or painters, as the Vermeer String Quartet had done, and they hit on a name with a very different story. As self-confessed cricket tragics, they chose Benaud. Their motto might be, 'If music be the food of love, play forward.'

The Melbourne group has since honoured its namesake by winning, among other distinctions, the Piano Trio prize at the Australian Chamber Music Competition and becoming a favourite choice of William Lyne, Emeritus Artistic Director of Wigmore Hall in London, one of the world's most renowned chamber-music venues. When Lyne discovered the provenance of the trio's name—that it really was Richie and not, say, the village of Benaud in the Auvergne, or some hitherto unsung composer—he was the more enchanted.

'These boys love cricket, but they come on stage and they're absolutely transformed, the music just takes over...I defy anybody to come into this hall and hear those boys playing and not become excited and moved and addicted to chamber music for the rest of their lives,' he said.

Lachlan Bramble, the Benaud Trio's violinist and also a member of the Adelaide Symphony Orchestra's indoor-cricket team, has explained that the group wanted a name totally distinct from classical music and its culture, history and protagonists. As cricket lovers, their answer was obvious. It was just a matter, no doubt, of what suited them best—the Chappell Trio, the Lillee Trio, the Thommo Trio…But Benaud was a clear winner, carrying the necessary dignity in the great concert halls of the world, and the Francophile hint of performance and style. So the Benaud Trio it was.

Apart from 'chin music' there seems not an immediate connection between cricket and melody, harmony. But wait! Neville Cardus, still generally regarded as the father of modern cricket writing, was a distinguished music critic who easily accommodated the two great arts—the one on the oval, the other in the concert hall or opera house.

When he appeared on the BBC's long-running radio classic *Desert Island Discs*—a program on which the guest nominates what music he or she would want to have if shipwrecked on a desert island—Cardus chose, among others, Schumann's Fantasie in C major, Wagner's 'Liebestod' from *Tristan und Isolde*, Beethoven's Symphony No. 4, Mahler's 'Song of The Earth', Schubert's Symphony No. 8 and Richard Strauss's Four Last Songs. These are the choices of a man of romantic and dramatic musical inclinations, and it was precisely these qualities of the romantic, the dramatic and the heroic that he brought to his writing about cricket. As the *Wisden* tribute to Cardus notes:

> To the enthusiast, cricket is romantic and in Mr Cardus's reports, the ordinary spectator saw his romantic and heroic feelings put into words for the first time. By

innovation and influence...he led thousands of people to greater enjoyment of the game...Before [the 1920s] there had been much competent cricket reporting, informed, sound in judgment, pleasant in manner. But the Cardus of the years shortly after World War I first brought to it the qualities of personalization, literary allusion and imagery. By such methods as presenting the contest between bowler and batsman as a clash not only of skills but of characters, he created something near to a mythology of the game.

Cardus's experiences with and particular loves in music deeply influenced his approach to his cricket writing, the style and tone with which he brought a game to life and his preferences within its infinite variations. He knew romantic heroes when he saw them. 'No team can be taken for granted as beaten before the match begins,' he wrote in the *Manchester Guardian* in 1956 on the eve of the Lord's Test, 'if it contains Harvey, Miller, Archer, Burke and Benaud,' and of Benaud he remarked in the same article, 'he is plainly gifted.' In 1953, Cardus says, Benaud, on his first visit to England, had displayed a 'kind of mastery. And what a man has done once,' he adds, 'he can do again.' Had he been around in Richie Benaud's palmy days, he might have been especially intrigued by Benaud's having followed his example in 'modern cricket writing' but also in having a peculiarly musical connection.

Lachlan Bramble theorises that playing music is in some

ways very similar to cricket. 'It's all about consistency of line and length, but sometimes you just have to hit it for six!' In early 2016, the Benaud Trio sadly saluted the passing of their namesake, Richie Benaud. They commissioned a special work—'Homage, a celebration of humanity through music'—by the award-winning composer and fellow cricket fan Iain Grandage, and coupled it with Schubert's epic and heroic Piano Trio in E-flat major, described by Robert Schumann as 'spirited, masculine and dramatic' and by contemporary critics as 'one of those shatteringly beautiful concert experiences that defies words'. Humanity, spiritedness, masculinity and intensely moving harmonies were combined by the group bearing his name to farewell Benaud in a guise removed from, yet evocative of, his world of sport and the idea of excellence of which Schubert, composing in the shadow of death, may have caught a last glimpse.

As for Benaud in the Auvergne, that 'delightful, quiet village' in the *département* Puy-de-Dôme in central France: it is a pretty enough place, with some of the dark and moody stonework typical of the volcanic region, but not at all as memorable or as striking as other parts of the Auvergne. In 1995, visiting my friend Jean-Paul Michelet, a literature professor at Clermont-Ferrand's Blaise Pascal University, it occurred to me that we were near enough to the village of Benaud to make a quick visit. This was really just a whim. Still, it was tempting; and now, twenty years on, it would be irresistible if I had the good fortune to be able to travel to the Auvergne once more.

You can drive on the A71 from Paris or go by train to

Clermont-Ferrand and on to Aurillac—a slow winding trip through many small villages and dark sombre forests until you arrive at Benaud. There would be no Benaud relatives, but there would be something of a frisson in walking down the narrow main street of the village of Benaud, fifteen thousand kilometres from the place where the name is legendary. But perhaps it would be easier to catch a Benaud Trio concert in Australia and enjoy the lateral Benaudian connections.

Anyway, two decades ago Jean-Paul could neither understand nor summon up much patience for my interest in the village of Benaud, which he did not find attractive and which was, in his considered view, inferior to most of the other wonders of the Auvergne. In any case, as I quickly discovered, his interest and pride in the Auvergne was gastronomically governed and Benaud, then at least, apparently did not have any diverting cuisine. So, in the end, bowing to his itinerary—he was after all my host—I didn't make the trip.

At the time I wasn't much bothered. It would only be years later that I would recognise my fascination with the existence of a village named Benaud in which there were no Benauds, as the renewal of a longstanding personal interest, perhaps a sturdy obsession. Benaud the village had its name and history long before Richie stood on its outskirts and posed by the village sign, though perhaps back in the remote Gallic past, the two—village and family name—had converged in some way.

The story grew beyond mere fortunately aligned nomenclature when Richie Benaud accepted an invitation to become the patron of France Cricket. In 1998 the country's status as a cricket-playing nation, formerly Affiliate, was raised by the International Cricket Council to Associate. Without doubt this promotion was influenced at least to some extent by the presence of such an illustrious patron.

As a resident, with Daphne, for some months every year in Beaulieu-sur-Mer on the Côte d'Azur, and with his French ancestry, Benaud did not find it odd to become a part of France's infant cricket organisation. France Cricket's salute to him and his own generous acceptance of the honour was not unusual in his later years. Nor could many of these recognitions be said to have been planned or consciously sought. Accolades, from an OBE through to the Cricket Hall of Fame, were woven seamlessly into the even tenor—or what appeared as such to all of us on the other side of the television screen—of Richie Benaud's days.

But even tenors are attained only after much organisation and hard work, though none of this might necessarily be evident to the casual observer. When in his playing days Benaud ran in to bowl with that fluid, purposeful action, he knew exactly where he wanted the ball to go, and most of the time that's where it went. He did this not by some unfathomable Benaudian act of will, but by meticulous planning, constant repetition and phenomenal dedication.

Bob Simpson, Benaud's successor as the Australian captain, who saw him close up, especially in the 1961 Ashes tour, says of him: 'His practise sessions on that tour had to be seen to be believed. He laboured long after other players had left practice; a lonely figure bowling with a youngster to retrieve the balls aimed at a handkerchief placed on a good length spot. His legendary accuracy developed here.'

And Alan Davidson, a lifelong close friend of Benaud's, and a team mate of his in, among other games, the Tied Test and the Old Trafford Test of 1961, fondly remembered their early days.

> He worked as a journalist in *The Sun* newspaper office and I'd catch the train to Central and we'd catch the tram to Anzac Parade together and walk with our gear to the SCG. On this particular day he asked, 'Why is it the English bowlers can put a ball anywhere they like?' The reason, he said, was because Alec Bedser bowled 1100 overs a year in his County season—and that wasn't counting Test Matches. We decided during that 1956–57 summer, which was a domestic season, that we'd bowl unchanged from 4pm until 6.30… unchanged…and, believe me, by the time you got to 6pm you saw stars and all sorts of things!…Richie, well, he reached the stage where he could bowl blindfolded. We went to Africa in '57–58 and both of us scored over 800 runs. He took 100 wickets, I took 72 and all of the work we'd done over that previous eight months made us what we were. Richie's view was the only way you could get accuracy was by bowling, bowling, bowling and working on technique.

Although it seemed that nothing could interfere with such iron will and unwavering resolve, it was all nearly brought undone by weakness of the flesh—in short, his spinning fingers. And this brings us back to the village of Benaud and its millennia-old, undulating lava runs of surrounding countryside which, long after Benaud's cricket-playing days, made its appearance on his cultural and geographical horizon.

It had an obvious interest for Richie Benaud but he may not have even heard of it when, on a New Zealand tour in February 1957, and preparing for a match against a combined South Canterbury, Mid Canterbury and North Otago team, he dropped into the pharmacist in the port town of Timaru. Timaru, like the Auvergnois village of Benaud, is in an area of volcanoes and its undulating rural surrounds were created many thousands of years ago by the erupting, aptly named Mount Horrible, long since quiescent but leaving a legacy, as in the Auvergne, of sombre, charcoal-dark stone.

The twenty-six-year-old Benaud, however, would not have been aware of the eerie volcanic connections between the village that was his namesake and Timaru, under Mount Horrible, where he was seeking medication for Dengue fever. The pharmacist, Ivan James, being a Timaruan, was possibly attuned to the behaviour of volcanoes. When Benaud consulted him, James noticed the eruptions of skin on his spinning fingers, which regularly and very painfully cracked under the constant stress of the rough seam and the abrasive action of running the fingers across it to produce leg-spin.

It was a critical, career-threatening problem for which Benaud had been seeking a remedy or amelioration for some time. And it hadn't helped that the veteran Australian spinner Colin McCool, one of the Invincibles, noticing the wreckage of Benaud's fingers after the New South Wales versus Queensland Sheffield Shield opener of the 1952–53 season, urged him to find a 'bloody way' to fix his fingers or forget about a career as a spin bowler.

McCool told him a story about his own rough and abraded fingers. Before the Fifth Test at the Oval in 1948, he had been trying to hide the damage from his captain, Don Bradman. Just before the Test match, unluckily for McCool, Bradman chose to sit beside him at breakfast and noticed the state of his spinning fingers. It cost McCool a place in the team.

In that opening Shield match of 1952 Benaud bowled thirty overs in the first innings and, when Miller enforced the follow-on, twenty-nine in the second, with figures of 3 for 90 and 2 for 118. There was an interesting oddity in that follow-on innings. Captaining New South Wales for the first time after Arthur Morris had been summarily sacked during his absence overseas—a typically insensitive administrative act in Benaud's view, but not at all unusual—Keith Miller gave everyone but the wicketkeeper a bowl in the second innings as the match headed towards an inevitable draw. But most important, as far as Benaud was concerned, his fifty-nine overs had once again focused attention on the apparently insoluble problem of his battered fingers—for which five years later Ivan James, the pharmacist of Timaru, having dealt with the Dengue-fever prescription, politely suggested a remedy.

Benaud describes being handed a small wide-mouthed bottle, a container with white powder and a piece of paper with the suggested remedy written on it. Desperate enough for anything, Benaud gave this 'long shot' a try and the treatment worked instantly. James was a genius in Benaud's grateful view. Benaud's fingers toughened up so that even prolonged bowling spells didn't produce cracking. And so, a hemisphere apart, each of them in the shadow of long-dead volcanoes and insignificant enough in the global scheme of things, the Auvergnois village of Benaud and the New Zealand port town of Timaru became geographical and, in their own quiet way, spiritual landmarks for Richie Benaud.

'Bowling, bowling, bowling' was Benaud's cricket solution, but it emanated from a more profound psychological and intellectual orientation. It was the way he dealt with most things. It was a strategy to gain control and mastery not in any overbearing, personal sense—his leadership on the ground and in the commentary box was careful and measured. Much of it was by example and, when explicit, mostly subtle—except perhaps for the time he reputedly told a very young James Packer rampaging around the commentary box to 'Fuck off, son.'

'He always had the ethics of cricket in his mind,' Alan Davidson said. 'There was never a scene with any of the players when he was captain. Never any ill-feeling, no bad behaviour. Whenever a bloke lost his cool and started to carry on, Richie said, "That'll be enough," and it stopped immediately. It was the happiest time I knew in cricket, because he moulded together a group of blokes who became a good team.'

'Bowling, bowling, bowling' is a metaphor for keeping at it, whatever the task or aspiration, and not only in the end getting it right but conquering it, mastering it. It seems that this approach was part of Richie Benaud's temperament, the way some people are perfectionists, and some lackadaisical no matter how hard they try or how often they resolve to be otherwise. But Benaud's carefully planned early moves, not in cricket but in the world beyond, introduced him to people whose attitude to their chosen field suited his temperamental inclination towards hard work, his conviction that effort, even if so often repeated that it at times verged on drudgery, was in itself a virtue, and that the mastery of an art, whether operatic, literary, balletic or athletic, was one of life's great goals.

It's easy to see all this playing out in his cricketing life and then, more so and for longer, in his career in the media. But there is one dimension of Benaud's achievement in which control and mastery take an unusual turn, namely in his writing. Benaud became a journalist because that was what he wanted to do. He didn't shun the dirty routine or unspectacular jobs, in order to experience the full gamut of the fourth estate's multitude of riches and sins. And with the prescience that would distinguish him both as player and media professional, he set about learning from the best in the business for what might be the requirements of later years.

But Benaud was also a writer. He had things to say that neither commentating nor day-to-day journalism would satisfactorily accommodate. Cricket was his passion and, as he says in his *Way of Cricket*, he had much to say about this 'finest' of games. He is feeling his way in this, his first book. He thinks of himself as a natural cricketer with a style long ago established, and basically unchanged and unchangeable. It is as if the rigid boundaries and protocols with which he imbues his cricket have also infused the writing itself.

Benaud encountered early on the truth of D. H. Lawrence's well-known bon mot about writing: 'If you try to nail anything down in the novel, either it kills the novel, or the novel gets up and walks away with the nail.' Nailing things down, getting them clear and under control, was part of the Benaud personal style, but in *A Tale of Two Tests* at least, the nail came unstuck to the benefit of the book. The no-nonsense attention to documentary truth and the rather stern insistence on the authorial voice with a more or less inflexible style are replaced by a talent for narrative, descriptive flair and a sensitive reading of atmosphere. The very title, with its glance to Dickens' *A Tale of Two Cities*, signals a creative heat behind the expected lineaments of a cricket book. In Dickens' famous opening lines—

> It was the best of times, it was the worst of times, it was
> the age of wisdom, it was the age of foolishness, it was
> the epoch of belief, it was the epoch of incredulity, it
> was the season of Light, it was the season of Darkness,

it was the spring of hope, it was the winter of despair,
we had everything before us, we had nothing before
us, we were all going direct to Heaven, we were all
going direct the other way

—the paradoxes, opposites, highs and lows, hopes rising and
hopes dashed dramatically prefigure the story of both the Tied
Test and Old Trafford. Like Dickens, Benaud understands the
passing observations that intensify atmosphere. The glimpsed
Manchester greyness and rain-slick roofs as he prepares to tell
the story of that Fourth Test at Old Trafford in 1961 graphically
evoke the cold drizzle and the low swirl of leaden cloud that
threatened and finally interrupted play on the first day. And
then there are the briefly noticed 'white flowers dotting the turf;
clover flowers' as he arrives for the last day of the Tied Test,
unmown flowers that would play such a role in the final, critical
moments of the game.

His tale of each Test captures all the drama, surprises, skills,
camaraderie and intensity of those amazing days of cricket in
Brisbane and Manchester. There is no lack of detail about the
tactics, skills and fluctuations of these matches, but their sense of
story and the underlying excitement of the teller of the story is
in the mode of fiction and has some of the freedoms of fictional
narrative.

When Davidson hits that huge 6 off Allen's last ball, Mackay
wonders if the ball might 'burst' when it hits the brick wall at
the railway line, and Davidson himself remembers it as 'such a

sweet hit'. But in *A Tale of Two Tests* the incident is so memorable that it can withstand the indulgence of retelling here. Benaud captures it as the ball rising and rising, seeming forever on the ascent, unreachable and unforgettable, until its wondrous trajectory is ended by that railway wall. In the ball's conquering wake, Benaud remembered most of all 'long off's despairing glance'— a splendid detail.

The tension in both accounts is handled with great assurance and effect. On the rest day at Old Trafford, with events already having run through confronting twists and turns that seemed to make a mockery of planning and tactics, Benaud writes, with a kind of shrugging disorientation, that he didn't give the game much thought on the Sunday—it wouldn't have done much good. He sounds like Albert Camus' hero, Meursault, in *The Outsider*. 'Mother died today. Or, maybe, yesterday; I can't be sure'; or perhaps a closer reference for an Australian reader would be Henry Lawson's 'It didn't matter much—nothing does' in the story 'The Union Buries its Dead'.

Of course it mattered a great deal, but Benaud's subtle implication is that they need in their different ways at least temporary respite from the grip of the game. Because, as he admits, there was no denying that they were all feeling tense about what the next day might bring, no matter how much they pretended otherwise.

A Tale of Two Tests includes 'Some Thoughts on Captaincy', as if Benaud felt he should straighten the record and return to his more characteristic—and perhaps more comfortable—discursive style. In his subsequent books, all of them important, lively contributions to the literature of cricket, the Benaudian control, the protocol of 'bowling, bowling, bowling', is reasserted. Narrative gives way, by and large, to essay and anecdote, discussion and occasionally polemic.

He does all this very well, but the creator in him, the storytelling verve, so much a part of *A Tale of Two Tests*, never again holds sway. It is why I would say that in the Benaud oeuvre *A Tale of Two Tests*, in which that immediately recognisable commentary-box style, timing and caution is least evident, stands out and is the best of them.

The dedication of *A Tale of Two Tests* reads: 'With many thanks to the 1961 Australian Team for providing the happiest months of my cricketing life.' Many happy months ensued in the next fifty years of his life in cricket, but the warmth and genuineness, the almost boyish pleasure that lies behind and informs that dedication, were typical of him then and remained characteristic, despite the greater gravitas that accompanied maturity, success, responsibility and fame.

Bill Lawry observes that Benaud's 'enthusiasm for a new star such as Lara or Warne was a joy to watch. He rarely criticised players, sometimes he was critical of administrators, but only with the interest of the game at heart.' Ian Chappell's gift bat was an early example of this enthusiasm, but there were many others, and none so fulsome and excited perhaps as his support for Shane Warne. In Warne, Benaud recognised not just another very accomplished leg-spinner, but a champion.

Recounting the story of how Warne had asked him for some advice while they were playing golf together, Benaud explains that he advised, as always, to 'keep things simple' and, above all, to perfect a leg-break that was fiercely spun, a stock ball that ripped, to use the spin bowler's jargon. And, he continued, Warne must learn to pitch that fierce spinner precisely, hitting the same spot time and again (bowling, bowling, bowling), and develop a versatility with it that would be attacking or defensive at will. Benaud warned, as he had often done in dealing with beginners, that this process would take about four years to complete. Warne, he recalled wryly, needed only two.

Benaud never evinced the slightest interest in Warne's off-field dramas; though, no doubt, to the extent that these events interfered with or cramped Warne's cricketing prospects—such as his chance of captaining Australia—Benaud must quietly have regretted them. Warne, after all, would have been, if the cards had fallen that way, not only captain of the Australian Test team but a leg-spinner captain.

In an essay called 'Being There' in *Anything But...An Autobiography*, Benaud devoted close attention to Warne's career, development and extraordinary skill, and predicted that, if Warne could recover satisfactorily from the shoulder operation he was about to undergo, he would captain Australia. For various reasons, some of them controversial, that didn't happen. But Warne's convoluted off-field script exerted no influence on Benaud, who saluted the famous leggy in *Anything But... An Autobiography* with a telling personal comparison. Benaud played 63 Tests and took 248 wickets. In his sixty-third Test, Warne took his three-hundredth wicket. Whatever the reliability or otherwise of some statistics, Benaud insists this particular one tells the true story, and the story was that Warne was a great champion, the best of his kind that Benaud, himself a champion in his day, had ever seen.

In an interview with Mark Nicholas, he bestowed on Warne the greatest possible accolade. Nicholas asked him, 'If you started again now as a young leg-spinner, what would you want?' To which Benaud answered, 'To be coached by Warne and to bowl at the other end in an attack with Warne.'

Hamlet's memory of his father—'He was a man, take him for all in all / I shall not look upon his like again'—is an often-used Shakespearean tribute. Another, lesser-known accolade, from Shakespeare's *Julius Caesar*, is Mark Antony's salute to the fallen Brutus: 'His life was gentle, and the elements / So mixed in him that Nature might stand up / And say to all the world, "This was a man."'

Each is a magnificent encomium, not least because both recognise that deserved and abundant praise must be cognisant of the flawed nature of humanity. Richie Benaud deserves both salutes because he, of all people, would have valued their relative reticence and their powerful sincerity.

BIBLIOGRAPHY

BOOKS BY RICHIE BENAUD

Way of Cricket (1961)

A Tale of Two Tests: With Some Thoughts on Captaincy (1962)

Spin Me a Spinner (1963)

The New Champions: Australia in the West Indies, 1965 (1966)

Willow Patterns (1969)

Test Cricket (1982)

World Series Cup Cricket, 1981–1982 Season (1982)

The Hottest Summer: World Series Cup Cricket, 1982–1983 Season (1983)

The Ashes 1982–83: Australia v England (1983)

Benaud on Reflection (1984)

The Appeal of Cricket: The Modern Game (1995)

Anything But…An Autobiography (1998)

My Spin on Cricket (2005)

Over But Not Out: My Life So Far (2010)

SELECT BIBLIOGRAPHY

Alex Buzo and Jamie Grant (eds), *The Longest Game*, Mandarin Press, 1992

Steve Cannane, *First Tests: Great Australian Cricketers and the Backyards that Made Them*, HarperCollins, 2010

Richard Cashman, *The 'Demon' Spofforth*, University of New South Wales Press, 1990

Gideon Haigh, *Mystery Spinner: The Story of Jack Iverson*, Text Publishing, 1999

Gideon Haigh, *The Summer Game: Cricket and Australia in the 50s and 60s*, ABC Books, 2006

Gideon Haigh, *On Warne*, Hamish Hamilton, 2012

Gideon Haigh, various articles provided to the author

Murray Hedgcock (ed.), *Wodehouse at the Wicket: A Cricketing Anthology*, Hutchinson, 1997

Brett Hutchins, *Don Bradman: Challenging the Myth*, Cambridge University Press, 2002

C. L. R. James, *Beyond a Boundary*, Hutchinson, 1963

Mike Marqusee, *War Minus the Shooting: A Journey Through South Asia During Cricket's World Cup*, Heinemann, 1996

Greg de Moore, *Tom Wills: His Spectacular Rise and Tragic Fall*, Allen & Unwin, 2008

Louis Nowra, *Warne's World: A Personal Appreciation of Shane Warne*, Duffy & Snellgrove, 2002

Peter Roebuck, *It Takes All Sorts: Celebrating Cricket's Colourful Characters*, Allen & Unwin, 2005

Christian Ryan, *Golden Boy: Kim Hughes and the Bad Old Days of Australian Cricket*, Allen & Unwin, 2009

Rob Steen, *Floodlights and Touchlines: A History of Spectator Sport*, Bloomsbury, 2014

Rob Steen, personal papers and correspondence provided to the author

Mark Taylor, *Time to Declare*, Ironbark, 1999

Steve Waugh, *Out of My Comfort Zone: The Autobiography*, Viking, 2005

Charles Williams, *Bradman: An Australian Hero*, Little, Brown, 1996

Robert Winder, *Hell for Leather: A Modern Cricket Journey*, Victor Gollancz, 1996

ONLINE SOURCES

Richie Benaud on leg-spin: youtube.com/watch?v=nW1fRPqsa-A (part one of four videos)

On the mechanics of spin bowling: Rod Cross, 'Physics of Cricket', physics.usyd.edu.au/~cross/cricket.html

On players' reactions during, and reminiscences of, the Tied Test: Brydon Coverdale, 'If I'd Been Usain Bolt I Wouldn't Have Made My Ground', espncricinfo.com/magazine/content/story/491922.html

On the Tied Test, as seen by Alan Davidson: Kersi Meher-Homji, 'Birthday Boy Davidson Recalls Famous Tied Test', theroar.com.au/2010/06/13/birthday-boy-davidson-recalls-famous-tied-test and Brydon Coverdale, 'The Most Incredible Game', espncricinfo.com/thebig_2000_test/content/story/521054.html

On the fate of the Benaud family home: articles in the *Parramatta Advertiser* (dailytelegraph.com.au/newslocal/parramatta) throughout August–September 2010 and concluding in 2011, when the preservation campaign had failed

Geoff Lemon on the commentary box without Benaud:
'Just Not Cricket: How Channel Nine Is Destroying
a Legacy', theguardian.com/sport/blog/2015/feb/13/
channel-nine-destroying-cricket-legacy

Alan Davidson's recollections of early days with Benaud:
Daniel Lane, 'Richie Benaud Dead: Why He Was One of
the Greatest Cricket Captains', smh.com.au/sport/cricket/
richie-benaud-dead-why-he-was-one-of-the-greatest-
cricket-captains-20150409-1mi0is.html

ACKNOWLEDGMENTS

My special thanks to Gideon Haigh, Ashley Mallett, Rob Steen and Glenn Turner for their generosity with conversations, anecdotes, documentation and advice.

Also for various important kinds of help and encouragement I thank, among many: Murray Bramwell, Sam Childs, John Harms, Rick Hosking, Sue Hosking, Kim Hughes, Philip Hughes, Philip Jarvis, David Matthews, Patrick Matthews, Jane Novak, Huw Richards, John Timlin, Cameron Waring.

My thanks to the team at Text, especially Michael Heyward and my editor, David Winter.

And, as ever, and always, to Jane Arms.